KEY ISSUES IN EDUCATION AND TE

Also available from Cassell:

John Beck: *Morality and Citizenship in Education*

John Beck and Mary Earl: *Key Issues in Secondary Education*

Asher Cashdan and Lyn Overall (eds): *Teaching in Primary Schools*

Christopher M. Clark: *Thoughtful Teaching*

L.B. Curzon: *Teaching in Further Education: Fifth Edition*

Graham Haydon: *Teaching About Values: A Practical Approach*

Trisha Maynard (ed.): *An Introduction to Primary Mentoring*

Andrew Pollard: *Reflective Teaching in the Primary School: 3rd Edition: A Handbook for the Classroom*

Andrew Pollard (ed.): *Readings for Reflective Teaching in the Primary School*

Andrew Pollard and Pat Triggs: *Reflective Teaching in Secondary Education*

Jasper Ungoed-Thomas: *Vision of a School: The Good School in the Good Society*

Key Issues in Education and Teaching

John Wilson

CASSELL

London and New York

Cassell
Wellington House
125 Strand
London WC2R 0BB

370 Lexington Avenue
New York
NY 10017-6550

First published 2000

British Library Cataloguing-in-Publication Data
A catalogue record for this book is available from the British Library.

ISBN 0-304-70629-9 (paperback)

Typeset by York House Typographic Ltd, London
Printed and bound in Great Britain by Redwood Books, Trowbridge, Wilts.

Contents

Acknowledgements

The readings on each topic have been compiled from material arising from many years' discussion. Some of them, or part of them, have appeared elsewhere, particularly in the *Journal of Philosophy of Education*, the *Journal of Moral Education*, the *Oxford Review of Education*, *Taking Education Seriously* (Althouse Press), *A New Introduction to Moral Education* (Cassell), and *Philosophy and Practical Education* (Routledge and Kegan Paul). I should like to make acknowledgements to these, and also to those many students, teachers and tutors who have contributed to discussions with me over many years, to whom I owe a great debt of gratitude.

Introduction

Initial teacher education is now largely controlled and delivered by the schools, and not by universities or colleges: that is already true of the UK and USA, and there is a clear trend in that direction in most other societies. This presents the schools with an enormous and difficult task, in which this book attempts to assist them.

Most teachers – certainly all those with whom I have worked during the last 30 years – believe that becoming a good teacher or a good educator of pupils is not just a matter of apprenticeship. As well as picking up the craft of the classroom by observation and practice, student teachers also need to do some hard thinking about major educational issues. For, however dictatorial the authorities in government or elsewhere may be, it is inevitably the teachers themselves who will have to deal with such issues as equal opportunities, multicultural education, gender, discipline, moral education and many others. These are not easy issues to resolve, and student teachers will need a good deal of help from more experienced colleagues if they are to be able to think about them with the rigour they deserve.

Most teachers, again, would not wish to revert to the old system by which students, in some university department or college, were expected to absorb large chunks of the philosophy, psychology and sociology of education via a programme of mass lectures, which were often far too disconnected from actual practice in schools. But at the same time they are fully aware that the issues in question are both difficult and controversial, and lead fairly directly to problems which inevitably have philosophical, psychological and sociological aspects. These disciplines themselves are far from irrelevant. Teachers may have neither the time nor the resources to deliver them in any thorough or large-scale way – nor may this be necessary – but they must be able to show their relevance to student teachers if they are to do them any sort of justice.

Teachers' own professionalism depends largely on this. For the idea of a profession rests on a sophisticated professional judgement, informed not only by experience but also by clear and rigorous thinking, about major educational issues. The autonomy that should accompany such professionalism – the freedom of teachers to run their own show – depends similarly on their being able to display such sophisticated judgement, which alone gives them the right to be trusted. So in taking on the task of training or educating entrants to the profession, their own professionalism is also at stake.

The first point for teachers to appreciate, then, is that these issues require some sort of disciplinary input: that the questions arising in each topic will often be philosophical or psychological; that one cannot just 'discuss' or 'investigate' a topic as a whole, but must rather consider it from the viewpoint of the relevant disciplines. As Professor Hirst has emphasized (Hirst and Peters, 1970) we cannot just ask questions about 'sex' or 'cathedrals' as a whole: the questions will always be about the morality of sex, or the biology of it, or the emotions involved in it; about the aesthetic merits of a cathedral, or the engineering of it, or its use as an institution. Any question will be of a certain logical type, and fall within a more or less recognized discipline or kind of enquiry, where certain considerations are relevant and others irrelevant. So it is with educational topics: questions about them will be conceptual questions about the philosophy of (for instance) the curriculum, or empirical questions about the psychology of it, or about sociology relevant to it, and so on. Recognition of this is necessary for any serious enquiry.

This, rather obvious, point and its implications are apt to be resisted, if not in the theory or rhetoric of teacher education institutions, at least in their practice, for a number of reasons. Time is short: mentors, tutors and students are all understandably concerned with 'practical experience'; and those in control of teacher education programmes may themselves be ignorant of any of the educational disciplines and hence somewhat dismissive of their importance. There is a big gap between the rhetoric of 'delivering the disciplines via educational topics' (or the notion of 'the reflective practitioner') and the actual content of the programme, so that students obtain little real experience of tough-minded intellectual enquiry within any discipline at all. Moreover, even if the task is taken seriously, we cannot expect that all mentors and tutors (or indeed any one individual) can be expert in all the disciplines.

In other words, though the delivery system of this general knowledge and understanding may be a great improvement – in particular, the decentralization of students away from mass lectures into smaller groups with tutors whom they know more intimately, and the closer connection with school practice – nevertheless there is a danger that the *content* of what is learned may be less rigorous, and taken less seriously, because the disciplines are no longer so visibly institutionalized or perhaps so well understood. Placed in this position, mentors, tutors and students urgently need some guidelines to help them in this difficult task; and this book attempts to offer such help.

The book is intended primarily for students, mentors and tutors involved in initial teacher education, but not solely for them: in-service teachers confront the same topics and require the same sorts of understanding, even if their experience has given them more sophistication. It is based on a good many years' experience as a general tutor dealing with such topics, particularly in the context of the 'internship' scheme developed by the Oxford University Department of Educational Studies and other institutions, a model which has helped to change the nature of initial teacher education along the lines mentioned above. That sort of scheme is fast becoming the norm; so that I may reasonably hope that the book will be of use to all mentors, teachers, intending teachers, and teacher educators who find themselves, as we all do, in need of some guidance.

The nature and composition of the chapters in this book are unusual, and I must explain what I have tried to do. Rather than attempt to compile some sort of interdisciplinary symposium on each topic – really an impossible task, and one which would make the book far too long for practical purposes – I have collated material arising from discussions and seminars held with student teachers and practising teachers over many years, and from other informal discussions. Each topic has been the subject of many such discussions, and in the course of these the key points, concepts and attitudes related to each slowly began to become clearer: so that much of what we said could be rendered down, as it were, and brought out more sharply. They were the general concepts, values and principles to which the arguments always led us – sometimes fairly quickly, sometimes after traversing a good deal of ground.

It will be clear that I owe an immense debt to those who took part in such discussions. I mention this here because I want to stress that these compilations are not intended to represent simply my own views – though no doubt I may have unconsciously favoured these. In any case the reader is neither obliged nor even encouraged to agree with them, only to face them squarely. They have been compiled with an eye on (a) brevity and clarity, (b) the need to raise, in as sharp and challenging a form as possible, the basic questions of concept and attitude relevant to each topic, and (c) the need to be as free as possible from entrenched ideological postures. A series of questions for discussion and suggestions for further reading is given at the end of the book.

I should be sad if these general points were not faced by the reader, since that is the whole purpose of the book. However, one may go in various directions when they are faced. One may want to relate the points to practical experience in school or elsewhere: and some of the questions at the end of the book try to help with this. Or one may want to pursue the points further in the abstract, so to speak: and some of the questions are relevant to this enquiry. It would be quite wrong of me to dictate, perhaps even to suggest, which way the reader wants to go: though it seems to me that all of the three ways mentioned in the Postscript at the end of the readings are useful and profitable. The book will have succeeded in its purpose if it at least helps readers to pursue their interests in the light of pure reason.

My choice of topics is inevitably controversial. In some countries there are government-sponsored bodies (the TTA [Teacher Training Agency] in the UK, for instance) that now dictate a number of topics to institutions of teacher education, thereby exercising a centralist and *dirigiste* control which seems itself questionable. That fact, together with the fashionability of certain topics, offers one criterion for selection. Another, rather more respectable, criterion is whether or not a topic is something which all teachers, in any society at any time, will certainly have to face in practice; and yet another, in my judgement the most important of all, is whether a topic is central to the enterprise of education as such (rather than to other enterprises, such as politics). Fortunately there is a considerable overlap when these three criteria are applied, and I hope to have been able to do some justice to them all. Nevertheless there are tensions between them, and the question of what topics ought to be on the agenda for teacher education would itself offer excellent material for a seminar. I have tried throughout at least to choose topics which will be relevant to problems basic to all education, rather than those which merely illustrate prevailing fashion.

The chapters fall into four main groups. In Part I we look at the enterprise of education itself and its implications, including the implications for teacher education, and at some of the psychological attitudes which we may bring to it. In Part II we consider some issues about the curriculum, the teaching of subjects, and motivation. Part III is concerned with the school as a community: with discipline, personal and social education, selection and competition. In Part IV we discuss some important political or social issues which are relevant to practical education, such as gender, race, equality and handicap. (Of course, many of these issues interlock and overlap.) That seems to me to represent at least one fairly natural ordering of the topics, but each piece (as well as each Part) can stand on its own, and there is no requirement on the reader to follow the above order.

Each topic in itself generates a good many basic questions, and I cannot hope to have done more than just to highlight some of them, often in a controversial and sometimes provocative form. There is no question of attempting to 'cover all the ground' or 'present a balanced and complete picture': many volumes would be required even to attempt such a task. Time for students both in initial training and on in-service courses is short: any book such as this can do no more than give the reader some taste for (and, I hope, commitment to) the hard intellectual pursuit of the very complex and important issues that the study of education necessarily embraces. It is to be hoped that readers will wish to pursue those issues for themselves in the future.

Part I

The enterprise of education

Chapter 1

What education is

We start with some simple propositions:

1. There are a number of human enterprises, distinguishable from each other, that we classify under such headings as 'medicine', 'art', 'education', 'science', and so on.
2. These enterprises characteristically have different purposes and aim at different kinds of goods: because of this their methods of procedure, governing rules, and criteria for success are different.
3. In order to be practised successfully, or at all, each enterprise needs certain necessary conditions to be fulfilled ('necessary', because there is a logical connection between the conditions and the enterprise).
4. It is always possible, and very often happens, that an enterprise is neglected, misunderstood, eroded, obliterated, overridden or in some way damaged or corrupted by particular circumstances.

We keep these propositions simple and general because we want to avoid complex questions about what is to count as the proper way of distinguishing between one enterprise and another, what particular verbal markers (the titles of each enterprise) normally mean in various languages, what are the nature and details of the necessary conditions, and any other sophisticated problems that might be thought relevant. We will just say that if someone were to maintain, for instance, that there is *no* way of satisfactorily distinguishing between 'medicine' and 'art', that medicine does not aim at goods (e.g. health) different from those that art aims at, that there are no necessary requirements for the successful practice of medicine (even the ability to inspect a patient's body and to treat it physically) or that certain circumstances might not make it difficult or impossible for medicine to flourish, we do not want to argue with him or her here.

Ought we to start, then, by defining education? Something turns here on what is to count as 'defining'. Many people nowadays are reluctant, perhaps with some justice, to talk about the definition, or the 'essence', of education; and it is true that a very great deal has been written under headings like 'The aims of education', 'The nature of education', 'The concept of education' and so forth, most of which is more confusing than helpful. It is better to start by asking ourselves what it is that such discussions are attempting to clarify, why we need to consider the 'concept' or the 'nature' of education. Suppose we are teachers, or educational administrators, or researchers, or civil servants in some Ministry of Education: what is the point of engaging in reflection about education?

To this question the answer is reasonably clear; it is, quite simply, so that we can have an adequate and consciously held view about what we are trying to do, about the nature of the enterprise in which we are engaging. Now, of course, actual people in actual jobs – teachers, civil servants and so on – will be engaged from time to time in many different enterprises. Teachers do not only teach: they may keep the register, referee football matches, attend union meetings and so on. Similarly, doctors do not only cure people: they may also have to fill in forms, keep accounts, tidy the consulting-room and all sorts of other things. But we (rightly) have the feeling that there is some enterprise with which these people are, or ought to be, specially connected, something that is central to what they do. Just as doctors are concerned primarily with medicine and promoting health, so (we may feel) teachers and others are, or ought to be, primarily engaged in the enterprise of educating.

This feeling, so far vaguely expressed, does not allow us to conclude that the other enterprises are unimportant or ought somehow to be got rid of. Plainly, much will depend on circumstances. If we are attacked by barbarians or have not enough to eat, it will no doubt be sensible for teachers (and perhaps even doctors) to stop teaching (curing) and turn their attention to finding food for themselves and other people or to fending off enemy attacks. The feeling is rather that there are *in principle* – 'in theory' if you like, though we hope also in practice – enterprises whose nature just *is* different. Educating people is one thing; curing them is another; keeping them properly fed is yet another; and so on. We have different words that fairly mark these enterprises ('education', 'medicine', 'economics'), but the words in themselves may not give us a sufficient grasp of what the enterprises are and how they differ from each other. For the enterprises exist in their own right ('in principle' or 'in theory'): whether or not people identify them or practise them at all, they would still be important; the enterprises we call 'science', 'medicine', and 'democracy' are important in themselves, even though many societies may have had no understanding of them and lived by superstition, witch-doctoring and tyranny.

There are two general temptations that need special notice. The first lies in identifying an enterprise that exists in its own right with particular social practices or institutions. To take a parallel: human beings may engage in an activity or enterprise that we may want to call 'religion' (though, no doubt, we are not entirely clear just what this enterprise is). It would be wrong to think that this is the same as saying that certain people and social practices – parsons, funerals, churches and so on – actually exist or even that there are certain sets of beliefs and doctrines which are called 'religious'. For we could always ask, 'Are these people (institutions, beliefs etc.) whatever they may be *called*, actually concerned with religion?', and we may often find that they are not. If we identify religion with certain social practices, we make the same mistake as the person who is humorously quoted as saying, 'When I say religion of course I mean the Christian religion, and when I say the Christian religion of course I mean the Church of England'. The point is not just that such people are prejudiced: it is that they have no idea of religion as an enterprise in its own right.

So it is with the notion of educating people. We may call certain things 'schools' and certain people 'teachers'; and we may say that what we are doing is to educate children, but we have to be able to show that this is, in fact, what we are doing. The mere existence of social practices with the word 'education' attached to them indicates nothing; any more than, in the police state of Orwell's *Nineteen Eighty-Four* (1949), the existence of an institution called 'The Ministry of Truth' proved that the institution was, in fact, concerned with truth (rather than, as Orwell represents it, with propaganda). It is a very open question how much actual education goes on in those institutions that we currently classify under that heading. Clearly, we cannot answer the question until we know, or decide, what 'education' is to signify; but equally we cannot assume that the answer is provided by existing institutions.

The second temptation is to use (or abuse) 'education' to endorse not a particular set of social practices but some particular ideal or set of values that we happen to favour. Most writers on the subject have some general ideology, or 'doctrine of man', or political or moral theory that they want to sell, and their 'educational theory' (together with what they want 'education' to mean) exists chiefly as a kind of spin-off, so to speak, from this general idea. Thus Plato (*Laws*, pp. 643–4, original emphasis):

> When we abuse or commend the upbringing of individual people and say that one of us is educated and the other uneducated, we sometimes use this latter term of men who have in fact had a thorough education – one directed towards petty trade or the merchant shipping business, or something like that. But I take it that for the purpose of the present discussion we are not going to treat this sort of thing as 'education'; what we have in mind is education from childhood in *virtue*, a training which produces a keen desire to become a perfect citizen who knows how to rule and be ruled as justice demands. I suppose we should want to mark off this sort of upbringing from others and reserve the title 'education' for it alone.

A very large part of Plato's educational theory, in the *Republic* and elsewhere, is devoted to this particular goal: that is, to turning out 'perfect citizens' in the interests of a well-ordered state.

It is worth noticing here that it is not just the English word 'education' that tempts us to move in one or the other of these two directions. Other words in other languages suffer the same fate: thus Plato, in the passage above, monopolizes the Greek word *paideia* (here translated as 'education') for his particular purposes; and the same can be, and has been, done with the French *éducation*, the German *Bildung* and so forth. The same temptations beset words (in any language) that signify enterprises of a fairly general nature, which we have not taken the trouble to get clear: 'religion', 'politics', 'morals' and many others. They lure us to endorse either existing social practices or else our own partisan views (and, indeed these two may obviously be connected with each other more closely than we have here made apparent).

So far as we can see, these and other similar manoeuvres are not only mistaken but largely unnecessary. There is a concept that, when properly explained, makes tolerably clear the kind of enterprise we need to distinguish and (though this is, in one way, a secondary consideration) best fits the term 'educate' as it is now normally used by English-speakers and other parallel terms that exist in other languages. To state this as briefly as possible: 'education' is the marker for a particular enterprise or activity, which has as its aim or 'good' the sustained and serious learning of rational creatures, planned in some coherent or overall way. We educate people (rather than treating them in other ways) when we are engaged in bringing such learning about, and people become educated when, or in so far as, they have done some learning of this kind.

Compared with the particular pictures presented by most authors, this is a fairly broad concept, but it is the concept that most contemporary English-speakers mark by the term 'education'. There is some limitation on what learning will count as education. We do not use the term of trivial or fragmentary bits of learning, nor of the learning of animals or infants, but we do use it where what is learned may be undesirable (bad habits, hatred of Jews or plenty of other things) and where the amount of knowledge or understanding is very small (one can learn, in a serious and sustained way, to acquire certain habits, or skills, or attitudes without much knowledge attached to them). We speak of *bad* (that is, not just incompetent but evil) education – just as we can speak of bad religion, bad moral principles, bad political ideals and so on: we have to distinguish these from cases that are not cases of religion, or morality, or politics at all – and also of education that does not involve much knowledge or understanding.

This (very brief) sketch needs to be supplemented by two elaborations. First, some limitation, not so much of content as of general intention, is placed on the concept of education by virtue of the fact that education is a general or comprehensive kind of enterprise. Thus the *Oxford English Dictionary* speaks of 'education' as 'systematic instruction, schooling or training', and for 'educate' gives 'to bring up (young persons) from childhood so as to form [their] habits, manners, intellectual and physical aptitudes'. Not just any learning counts as education: the learning has to be seen as part of a systematic and coherent enterprise. Hence the grammar of 'to educate' is different from the grammar of (for instance) 'to train'. We can train people in particular skills, or for particular tasks, or as fillers of particular roles, but we can only educate *people as such*: if we claim to educate people, we claim to be viewing their learning from some general, overall or comprehensive point of view, not *just* with an eye to certain jobs or skills. It is also different from 'indoctrinate', 'socialize', 'school', 'teach' and many other such terms.

Of course, since people have minds, and since education consists of learning, it is likely that a large part of this enterprise will be seen as the development of knowledge and understanding in people; indeed, an educational ideal that involved no such development would be hard to conceive. Yet one might easily think that the really important things for people to learn – still in a comprehensive and coherent sort of way – did not involve much intellectual or 'cognitive' sophistication but were more in the area marked by 'character', 'habits', 'attitudes' and so forth: and one might believe that these things were best learned by imitation, or practice, or exhortation, or game-playing or other methods of that kind. Again, one might think it rash to lay down any particular content as being 'really important' for *all* pupils – such content might reasonably vary according to each pupil's particular needs, abilities or station in life. But the notion of education is neutral with regard to any questions of content; so long as there is an enterprise of this general kind, the term 'education' cannot be rejected.

Second, 'education' is normally a fairly formal, structured or institutionalized enterprise, something designed to raise people above the level of what they would naturally learn for themselves in the ordinary course of events. We do not speak of parents and other language users educating their children, or even teaching them to talk, if the children just pick up the use of language from the adults – even though this learning may be thought crucially important for any mental development. We may, indeed, loosely say that certain people or experiences exercise an 'educational' effect, but 'educate' is a much narrower term than 'bring up', 'rear' or 'nurture'.

These are at least some of the issues that would emerge from a thorough and systematic study of how words are actually used. Much more work, in our judgement, needs to be done in this field, both on English words and on those terms that are, at least *prima facie*, parallel in other natural languages. But whatever may or may not be true of English and other usage, the important point is that a particular kind of enterprise exists that needs to be delimited in this way because it is concerned with a certain kind of 'good' – namely, learning. There are, of course, still wider concepts: 'upbringing', say, or 'what we do for children' would include a number of very different goods; at one time we are concerned with our children's health, at another with their appearance, and so on. Learning, though a broad enough idea, represents only one kind of interest; nor is this interest confined to children. A variety of other terms normally goes along with this particular interest; we would not refer to children as pupils, for instance, nor to adults as teachers unless we had this interest in mind.

There are other enterprises concerned with other specific goods, as we have already noted, and it is important to see that each of these is delimited or bounded in the same sort of way. Often this is clear to us: we know pretty well when we do something to a person for medical reasons, and we can distinguish these from educational or economic reasons. A sick man may have to retire from attending university or from his business: this may be good for his health but bad for his education or his pocket. Sometimes, partly because of a lack of clarity about the terms and concepts in question, we are less clear. But whatever we choose to label as 'politics', or 'morals' or (to take a currently fashionable term) 'ideology', we must, if these terms are to have any clear meaning, be able to distinguish a political (moral, ideological) reason for doing something from another kind of reason, which means that we must be able to distinguish it from an educational reason.

In fact, if we resist the temptation to extend terms like 'political' ('moral', 'ideological', etc.) to cover more or less any consideration, we can already do this in many cases. It is politically desirable that when attacked by barbarians we should not worry too much about learning things but should devote our attention to keeping our society safe. It is morally desirable that if Romans are in danger of being burned alive, we should at least put off learning the violin until we have done what we can to help them. It is, or may be, 'ideologically' desirable (though we are not entirely clear what 'ideologically' means) that children from different social backgrounds should belong to the same school or the same housing estate; but whether this improves these children's learning may be another matter.

It is for these reasons that the concept of education, as we have tried to delimit it, cannot sensibly be seen as 'contestable', 'dependent on one's ultimate values' or anything of that kind, any more than can the concept of medicine, with its connected good (health). Indeed, we can go somewhat further than this. The enterprise of education is plainly necessary for any human society or individual, a point largely masked by those authors who prefer to adopt a much more stringent and value-impregnated concept and have to try to 'justify' it. The reason is that we could not come to resemble anything much like human beings or rational creatures unless we had done a good deal of serious and sustained learning, and it is implausible to suppose that such learning could be successfully done if we were left entirely to chance and nature. Some general or overall attempt, on a more or less broad front, to advance children's learning – whatever we may think it important to learn – seems essential if only because natural ability and circumstances are unreliable. In much the same way, an enterprise devoted to keeping people fit and healthy (that is, medicine) will be an inevitable feature of almost any society, even if different societies vary in their ideas of what counts as fitness or health, as they certainly vary in their ideas of how to achieve it.

Whether or not this sort of delimitation is acceptable as a definition of education does not ultimately matter all that much as long as we are clear about, and agree on, what verbal markers we are attaching to which enterprises. Few people will deny the importance of sustained and serious learning, even though they might dispute the delimitation, and even though they might disagree about what ought to be learned. But we are not always as clear as we should be about the logical or conceptual requirements that the notion of sustained and serious learning itself imposes on us and that we have to attend to if our educational practice is to prosper. There is a real danger that, under pressure from other (non-educational) sources, teachers and educators may lose their grip on what must surely be regarded as central to the notion of education.

Chapter 2

Enemies of education

There are two general ways in which an enterprise can be corrupted: by external pressure and by internal corruption.

1. *External pressure*   It may be that because of external pressures or desires that conflict with the enterprise, 'society' – or some group of power holders – does not give the necessary powers to those who should be conducting it. If, for example, administrators and porters do not allow doctors the scope and power necessary to conduct operations and otherwise treat their patients as the doctors think best, to that extent medicine is impossible. Similarly, if there is no class of people who are empowered to educate – who are charged with the making of educational decisions and trusted to use the time and money involved as they think best without fear of outside pressure – education becomes difficult or impossible. If a Gestapo agent, or a Party commissar, or a 'democratic consensus', or an educational fashion, or parental or bureaucratic pressure is breathing down the necks of educators and telling them what to do, they cannot do their jobs satisfactorily. The position becomes impossible for the enterprise, just as chess-playing cannot flourish if politicians tell chess players what moves to make.

   The people most plausibly to be identified as educators, and therefore to be given the relevant powers, are the *teachers* (in schools and universities) because, briefly, they have a better grasp of the knowledge and other things to be learned and they are personally familiar with the students who are doing the learning. We do not, of course, deny that both parents and society have some rights here – for instance, to choose schools for their children or to insist that students at least learn to be economically and socially viable – but within certain fairly obvious limits the enterprise must be conducted by those on the spot and in the know. The educators must have whatever disciplinary powers they need: sufficient powers to order the curriculum, the organization of the school and the methods of teaching; powers over the spending of whatever money society can afford to devote to education; powers to ensure the sanctity and potency of the school (college, university), if necessary in the teeth of society or political pressures; and powers to ensure the educability of their pupils (which include at least certain powers over the home environment). All these seem notoriously lacking in our society – and indeed in any society we know of; this is an interesting and important fact.

2. *Internal corruption*   Even if these powers are granted, it is always possible, of course, that the educators themselves may lose a proper grip on their own enterprise. They may become corrupted by various types of irrationality. A great deal of what passes for 'educational theory' or 'educational research' betrays this corruption. It arises chiefly from various fantasies about the human mind, which issue in forms that are, or should be, well known: a belief in behaviourism and 'behavioural objectives', the regarding of almost any attribute as a 'skill', an addiction to ideology, an obsession with equality and social class, and the characteristically liberal and paranoid guilt that makes us dismiss or play down ideas marked by 'punishment', 'examination', 'competition' and 'segregation' (ideas that at root encapsulate necessary features of any serious learning and any serious institution devoted to learning). Equally education may become corrupted by the authoritarian desire to *indoctrinate* pupils with some kind of ideology – 'Christian (Marxist, Islamic, democratic, etc.) values', or whatever.

Human beings are susceptible to these fantasies and types of irrationality in any social system; indeed, social systems usually do no more than echo and institutionalize the types of fantasy to which all individuals are liable. It is important to ensure that the external pressures are checked in order that education may have at least the chance of flourishing, but it is equally important that the tendencies to internal corruption are also checked in order that it may actually flourish. For that reason we believe that, however much light may be shed on the external, sociological or institutional forces that make education difficult, these forces will continue to flourish in one form or another so long as the basic fantasies continue to dominate us. It thus seems to be ultimately itself an educational issue; enough influential individuals need to understand the nature of the enterprise and its necessary conditions, and to gain sufficient control over their fantasies, to ensure that their intellects do not renege on what they have learned philosophically. This applies particularly to teachers themselves.

It is not surprising that education is today a natural stamping-ground both for political and bureaucratic pressure and for inner irrationality; there are obvious reasons why education tempts both earnest technologically minded bureaucrats and pseudo-idealists acting out their own compulsions. The really tiresome thing about this is that it masks the extent to which education, if allowed and encouraged to flourish, could change things for the better: an intuition that the 'great educators' of the past at least kept alive. If we could really teach people not only to be socially viable but also to become seriously attached to what is worth while, to conduct their moral lives with at worst competence and at best imagination and enthusiasm, to be able genuinely to love at least some other people (if only their own children), to find some genuine joy, excitement and contentment in life – if we could do any all or of these things, we should at least have some idea of the enormous power that education has in principle. That it does not wield this power in practice is not due primarily to lack of research or lack of economic or technological resources; it is due to the fact that we do not give the enterprise a fair chance.

Hence it is difficult, in this present age, to say very much about the positive possibilities of education: these sound futuristic or Utopian. In much the same way, it would have been difficult in the Middle Ages to talk of the 'wonders of science' or to make clear what benefits the properly constituted and fantasy-free practice of medicine would bring, because at that time these two enterprises were hemmed about with enemies that made their proper practice impossible. So it is with education now: it is apparent, here and there (in those rare cases where educators are both properly empowered and themselves uncorrupted), just how enormous are the benefits it can bring. In a (real if imprecise) sense, anyone who has ever had a loving parent or teacher knows well enough what education can do. But such cases are, regrettably, rare: we do not see many teachers with the influence of Socrates or Dr Arnold. (Who would hire Socrates nowadays? And would Thomas Arnold have tolerated the administrators and bureaucrats of today?) We have, as it were, a vague if precious glimpse of what education might be, if given a fair chance. That glimpse is worth hanging on to, though perhaps not much is gained by singing hymns to it. What we have to do, first and foremost, is to clear the ground – to understand ourselves and the enterprise – then we will have some chance of studying it, and conducting it, sensibly.

By far the most important thing here is to resist the pressure (whether from outside or from inside ourselves) *to impose our own values* on the enterprise. It is hard to avoid this, because we are tempted to regard them as non-controversial. 'Surely at least we believe in democracy and equality' – but then we remember that Plato and many other philosophers thought both democracy and equality to be pernicious. 'Surely at least in a Christian country ...' – but Christian values are also controversial. We have to eschew any moral (political, religious, bureaucratic) *content* for education. Quite apart from such content being controversial, our pupils (or some of them) will certainly want to challenge it: and then we either have to give it up, or else see ourselves as indoctrinators anxious to sell what we take as 'the right answers' rather than as educators encouraging pupils to think reasonably. Education has plenty of values, attitudes, concepts and practices *of its own* (to do with what is necessary for learning, knowledge and the improvement of reason): in trying to inject our own values we serve ourselves and minister to our own insecurity rather than to the enterprise itself.

Chapter 3

Educational studies and teacher education

It is difficult to write about educational studies without seeming either testy or despairing, because it seems that the crucial questions – questions about the basic nature and logic of such studies – are hardly ever raised, let alone answered. For one thing, the time never seems to be right. Thus economic recessions and other utilitarian or political pressures are often said to encourage reflection upon the nature, value and justification of such enterprises, but that is at best a half-truth; what actually happens is that the pressures change or rearrange the criteria of judgement, stressing – unsurprisingly and sometimes rightly – the instrumental, the utilitarian, the 'practical' and the 'relevant' (whatever these terms may mean). Those who negotiate on behalf of the enterprises have also to engage in a lot of fast footwork, as well as display prudence and political foresight, if their negotiations are to be successful; and that, though necessary, does not conduce to calm and leisured reflection. Conversely, in periods of euphoric expansion, like the 1960s in the UK and North America, few people are in a mood to think with any precision: they are too anxious to make hay while the sun shines, or not to get left behind in the gold rush.

Even when some effort is made, talk about educational studies (together with any decisions and actions taken about them) suffers from a difficulty which is also endemic to educational studies themselves. Briefly, there are many different kinds of questions involved – philosophical, sociological, historical, political, managerial, and so on. To make any serious progress towards answering some such overall questions as 'What ought educational studies to look like, and how can we get them like that?' we need the help of more than one discipline. Moreover, the lessons each discipline can teach us – the particular answers to the particular questions it addresses – cannot just be put side by side or somehow squeezed together (by the covers of a symposium, for instance): there is a proper *structure* required if our thinking is to be more than just intellectual amusement. Thus, we might reasonably suppose that we need to begin with some kind of conceptual or philosophical clarity about the particular nature of educational studies (as against other kinds of studies), and what that nature logically involves; then move to what the empirical disciplines can tell us about these studies, as practised by individuals and institutions; then turn to what, in the circumstances of the world as we now have them, we can actually do about improving matters. That is no more than a very broad outline of the required structure (the way in which what we have called 'the empirical disciplines' fit together, for instance, stands in need of much more investigation): but even this outline requires an effort of understanding and communication that we seem unable, or perhaps unwilling, to make. Hence, just as we talk breezily about 'integration' or 'interdisciplinary studies' in education itself but in fact make no coherent attack upon the problems involved, so in the enormous mass of literature on educational studies we see (for the most part) only the products of particular disciplines and approaches. Philosophers have something to say about the matter (e.g. Hirst, 1983; Wilson, 1975), but have often left it unclear how their conceptual points should be translated into action: on the other hand, those more concerned with the political world often produce interesting reportage of the current state of play, or practical suggestions of an *ad hoc* kind, but show little desire to consider the questions of concept or value which are logically prior to any sensible decision.

In such a situation it is hardly surprising that the most favoured approach tends to be pragmatic, managerial, and sometimes frankly opportunistic. Indeed there are perfectly good reasons for this. One is that Faculties (Schools, Departments, etc.) of Educational Studies are under much more pressure than most other segments of most universities, and under much more varied pressure – they have to spend more time keeping more people happy. Central government, state or local education authorities, teachers and teachers' unions are amongst the bodies that can exercise such pressure, and pressures of other kinds come from student demand (or the lack of it) and from the university or other central academic agency of accreditation. Another even simpler reason is that in a great many institutions educational studies and teacher education do in fact go on. Nobody is going to put these in cold storage until we have made up our minds what they ought to be doing, any more than schools will stop having timetables until debates about the curriculum cease (they never will). They have to be managed.

Even granted this, however, we begin to feel some worry. Admittedly certain people believe (or pretend to believe) that there are general truths of 'management' which are not simply banal ('It is important to be clear about your objectives') and which hold good irrespective of what is to be managed – whether one is managing General Motors, or a local drug store, or a love affair, or a nuclear power plant, or a Faculty of Educational Studies. Indeed this belief seems to be built into certain traditions: notoriously the amateur tradition of politics and the civil service in many countries, where high-grade managers are virtually interchangeable. But where such a tradition as this works well (and actually the framing and administration of educational policy is one of its more obvious failures), it is likely to be because of the (comparatively) high quality of the managers themselves rather than because there is a body of managerial theory which applies equally to education, espionage and the environment. It must, surely, make an important difference that we are managing education rather than something else.

We shall in fact try to show that education and educational studies are *sui generis* activities in a rather strong sense. If one considers seriously what it is actually like to educate people – the mere phenomenology of it, let alone the philosophical or conceptual implications – two things become apparent. First, education is not something entirely simple and material, like cake or money, which everybody can identify and evaluate and make decisions about without the need (at least normally) of expert opinion. Thus it has frequently been pointed out by philosophers that education cannot, for instance, be shared out equally (like cake) – it is not that sort of thing. It involves, centrally, some kind of human and at least semi-personal relationship, and is thus distinguishable from such standardized and packageable goods as food, housing, fluoridated water and (significant term) 'package' holidays in Jamaica. Secondly, however, it is not complicated in the way that nuclear physics and brain surgery are complicated: some people are better than others in education, but their expertise is not like that of the professional scientist – just as some people are better than others in various kinds of human relationships and activities, but not better because they understand more science. The kind of understanding is different.

If one is making educational decisions, then, or decisions affecting educational institutions, one can neither rely upon understanding or common sense possessed and deployed by everyone outside a lunatic asylum, nor rely on easily identified scientific experts, as one would if deciding on (say) nuclear power plants. And that puts education in the worst position. It is as if we had to rely on civil servants or other managers to tell us what to do about, for instance, marriage or morals or art or friendship or mental health or religion; and that is, or should be, frightening. For we feel, and are right to feel, basically *uncertain* about these areas: dimly aware that there must be criteria of goodness that apply to them, but uncertain about what they are.

Many people, perhaps particularly in societies where there are pressing needs of a practical or utilitarian kind – for more technology, better agriculture, improved physical health or whatever – may be inclined to doubt or dismiss these points. Such a reaction may well stem from justifiable motives; if our immediate need is to produce more engineers, or to defend the state against invasion, it can easily seem impractical, 'academic', 'irrelevant' or a mere luxury to consider the enterprise of education in its widest aspects. We have to teach our students to cope with these severely pragmatic demands, and (we suppose) have no time or need to enter upon more obscure matters. It is useful to spend a little time here in showing why that reaction, though not without weight, is dangerous and may be self-defeating.

Philosophers are accustomed to distinguishing 'education' from 'training' on the one hand and 'indoctrination' on the other. They do not, or should not, dispute the necessity (and in some circumstances the priority) of training: learning to survive has priority over the desirability of learning (say) about literature or music, and (though this is more doubtful) it may sometimes be necessary for psychological or political reasons to inculcate some particular creed or set of beliefs without subjecting them to the kind of independent criticism that the educator – as against the priest or the political commissar – wants to flourish. But education, though it may include these things, is not exhausted by them: to educate somebody is to be concerned with that person's learning in an overall sort of way – it involves treating him or her as an independent person, not just as someone who will do a particular job or be an unquestioning adherent of some particular creed. 'Educate' is the word we normally use, in English (there are equivalents in all other languages), for this broad task. But the point is not a linguistic one: the task *is there*, and we have to decide how important the non-training and non-indoctrinatory aspects of it are.

We are often inclined to underestimate these aspects and overestimate the utilitarian ones, for the following reasons:

1. Training in particular skills, and indoctrination into particular creeds, are *fragile*. The skills may rapidly become obsolete, especially at a time of swift technological change; and our pupils may react against and throw off the beliefs which we have inculcated, often with damaging and disruptive results.
2. The need for moral, social or political harmony is at least as great as the need for utilitarian skills, and its absence at least as damaging to society. The only secure and effective way of obtaining such harmony involves treating and educating our pupils as independent and autonomous people – they neither can nor ought to be bullied and forced into a particular mould.
3. The effective deployment of utilitarian skills itself depends on some degree of willingness and understanding on the part of individual people. There must be a background of general education – not only general intellectual competence and flexibility, but (to use an old-fashioned phrase) moral virtue which enables the skills to be pursued wholeheartedly and appropriately.
4. Education has to take into account the idea of a 'good life' for individual people; and though that 'good life' must obviously include a reasonable degree of material prosperity, it is arguable how high that degree needs to be. Standards of (material) living are important; but human happiness depends on many other things besides – being able to engage in personal relationships, having some sort of meaning in one's

life, coming to love and enjoy various worthwhile activities which are not a matter of economics, and so forth. These tend to be under-estimated because they are less visible and measurable (and also because most governments are less concerned with them).

It is in fact quite hard to believe, if we face the matter squarely, that any society is really indifferent to the non-training, non-indoctrinatory aspects of education. Parents and teachers are not *only* concerned that their children should earn a living and be comfortable: they want them to be happy and kind, to understand and enjoy something of the non-material goods that make life worth living, to appreciate the worlds of nature, art, music, science and so forth. No culture could devote itself exclusively, or even primarily, to turning out children who did no more than satisfy their material needs; it would be like trying to turn out a set of ants or robots or well-fed slaves or animals. Children are *people*, and remain people despite any efforts we may misguidedly make to the contrary. All that is (when we think about it, which it is sometimes quite hard to do in the face of utilitarian and political pressures) tolerably obvious. The trouble is that we are uncertain about how to proceed – how to educate, or what sort of education to provide. And this takes us back immediately to the question in which we are engaged: that is, the nature of education and educational studies.

It is roughly for these reasons that the first steps in establishing the credibility of educational studies are philosophical. Unfortunately the credibility, or certainly the force, of philosophy is itself not well established or understood. There is a story about a conversation between a philoso-pher and a commissar in Moscow, at a time when political dissidents were declared mad and sent to mental health institutions. The philosopher said words to the effect of 'You're cheating, because "mad" doesn't mean "dissident", hospitals are different from prisons, and mental health isn't the same as politics'. The commissar replied along the (familiar) lines of 'Oh, you philosophers, always talking about the meanings of words: we commissars have to be practical. Anyway, words and concepts are human products and we can make them mean what we like'.

A number of lessons should be clear even to the most doggedly anti-philosophical (or if not, nothing will be gained by further argument). The first is that the meanings of words and concepts do matter, in a quite practical way. The second is that these meanings are not variable at will, or in the service of political or ideological pressures (as in Orwell's *Nineteen Eighty-Four*), at least in the short term. In other words, the commissar was cheating, and cheating in a way which affected practical matters. The third lesson, in some ways the most important of the three, is that you do not have to be an expert philosopher, or not much of one, to grasp all this. How well you grasp it and how seriously you take it, is likely to be chiefly a matter of common sense, intellectual honesty and a certain kind of tem-perament. It is true, however, that if one were to enlarge on these criteria (particularly honesty), one would very soon want to say something about the Socratic idea of not claiming knowledge where in fact there is only confused opinion: that is, perhaps, in a broad sense philosophical. But it is of great practical importance as well.

If, then, anyone were to think (and many act as if they thought) either that we knew well enough what educational studies were and how we ought to pursue them, or that for practical purposes it did not matter whether we knew, it is not clear how one could profitably argue with him; for most of the relevant arguments would involve paying some attention to the meaning of words and the drawing of certain important distinctions – but it would be precisely that sort of thing that such people think unnecessary or unimportant, like the commissar. Perhaps one could goad them into discussion or reflection by little horror stories, like the one above; or perhaps some psychologist could tell us how to reassure them so that they could put their practical concerns, their immediate fears and desires, on the shelf for a bit, thus giving themselves at least the chance to reflect. Socrates' failure to deal with Thrasymachus – that is, with his feelings, not just his opinions – is still a model and instructive example here (Plato, *Republic*, 336 ff.).

Thrasymachus is relevant in another way too. For one of the things (or one interpretation of the things) he wanted to say was – putting it very broadly – that what counted as justice or moral virtue was *constructed* or *produced* in some way: as people commonly put it nowadays, a 'social product'. That reminds us of the commissar claiming that what counted as mental health, or politics, or any other enterprise was a 'human product' and that we could make the titles 'mean what we like'. It is fairly clear what is wrong with this. Differences, including the differences between human enterprises, exist not just in our minds but in the world. Looking after the health of someone's body is one thing, looking after his or her bank balance another, and looking after that person's appearance a third. These things simply *are* different – and they remain different whether or not individuals or societies understand or mark the differences. They are as different as chalk from cheese: and this has nothing to do with whether chalk or cheese are 'human products'.

If we now approach, cautiously, the credibility of educational studies, we can see clearly enough that a certain kind of credibility can be achieved by general managerial competence plus (if this is not already covered by 'managerial') the ability to 'sell' educational studies and the institutions that go in for them to the appropriate clients or customers; this latter being largely a matter of promoting those images – even that phraseology – which appeals to the customers at the time. Of course this is not only a valid but an essential activity; but the trouble with the credibility which it can achieve by itself is threefold, even if the practice thus advertised happens to be good. First, it is fragile and ephemeral. (Awareness of this partly accounts for the intense busyness, the desperate desire to be in the know and the swim, characteristic of many educationalists.) Secondly, unless the practice is based on what really *are* good reasons as against what is temporarily acceptable in certain circles, those outside the circles will not be convinced. But thirdly, what is of far greater importance, these moves do not establish the credibility of educational studies as such: they package and sell a certain line of goods – a certain style of research, certain brands of teacher training, perhaps certain appealing ideologies. In other words, the basic objection to seeing the establishment of credibility as centrally a matter of politics or public relations is this: it assumes, what is not true, that we know what educational studies are and how to pursue them – that we already have a good product, as it were, and need only to advertise and market it. However necessary it may be to proceed on this assumption in order to stay in business (particularly in hard times), it is a false assumption.

To enlarge a little on our present difficulties: because the criteria appropriate to pursuing education are not obvious, and because (in consequence of this) there are no agreed authorities or methods of procedure, educators tend to take their procedures and subject matter from the marketplace, so to speak. Fashionable topics are flung up from whatever is currently salient and well publicized, or from the current concerns of government or 'society' (whatever 'society' may mean). Similarly the lack of acknowledged expertise generates a style of doing business which is, necessarily, 'democratic', 'participatory' and in general egalitarian. It is not that these topics, or even (in some circumstances) this style, are always unimportant or improper; it is rather that educators seize upon them in desperation, and without any serious reflection about whether they are in fact appropriate. Education thus becomes politicized or – in a different sense of the word – 'socialized': that is, reduced to taking its cue from social or other concerns external to its own discipline or procedures.

For similar reasons, success (in the wordly sense of the term) in education is today largely a matter of good public relations. Where there are no well-established intellectual or other transcendental criteria, there are no (rational) authorities; the whole business becomes democratized and popularized, and rational authorities are replaced by ephemeral sages, trend-catchers, demagogues and ideologists. ('We're all in show-biz. now', as one professor of education once said to us.) Of course it is fatally easy either to hold some conspiratorial theory about this, whereby some well-organized (usually left-wing) group of people is supposed to be carefully and cunningly plotting the overthrow of traditional values; or else to take one's stand on a traditional (usually right-wing) ideology which is supported more by sentiment than rational or transcendental argument, or both. Indeed most of those who complain about modern education take up such mistaken options. Nevertheless, it is strikingly true that educational thought and practice is constantly changing: as with television programmes, the interest-rating in any particular project or movement inevitably drops after a comparatively short time, and the person who wants to succeed must develop a nose for the next fashion. Producing the right image becomes essential. This may be (slightly) less true of those in the higher echelons of educational studies, where (often inappropriate but more durable) images of scholarship and university-based criteria still prevail – though, with more and more democratized and politicized universities, even this is doubtful. But it is very obvious in the appointment of teachers and head teachers, in educational research, and in teacher training.

The nature of educational studies has been, and still is, reflected in constant attempts to assimilate it to one or another model. Not so long ago (and in some degree even now) the practical enterprise of education was taken as parallel to such enterprises as engineering or medicine. Of these latter it is demonstrably true that there exists a large and well-founded body of knowledge, fairly to be called 'theory', in the natural sciences – mechanics, chemistry and so forth. The training of practising engineers and doctors could thus plausibly be seen as partly the assimilation of the relevant theory, plus some experience of the practical aspects of engineering and medicine on building sites, hospital wards, or wherever. So, too, with the training of teachers: there was supposed to be – perhaps still is supposed to be – some grasp of 'educational theory', together with some admixture of 'practical skills'. A good deal of (fruitless) debate still persists about how to 'connect theory with practice' and about what the 'right mixture' of 'theory' and 'practice' should be.

There are a number of fairly obvious reasons why this cannot be right. One is that it is (to say the least) doubtful whether we have any very well-founded body of *knowledge* which could fairly be called 'educational theory': that is, sets of true propositions which are significantly above the level of common sense or what intelligent people could pick up for themselves with a bit of experience, and which are clearly relevant to the practical enterprise of education. Another, more central reason, is that there are plainly excellent teachers who are wholly ignorant of such 'theory': something that could not happen in engineering or medicine. When teaching and education go wrong, it is again (to put it conservatively) not at all clear that this is because our psychological or sociological theories are not sophisticated enough: indeed, it is more likely because we have certain personal or ideological prejudices which we wrongly dignify with the name of 'theory'.

Some dim perception of this was no doubt a part-cause of a sharp change in fashion in the direction of the 'practical'. Disenchanted with innumerable lectures on the philosophy, psychology, sociology etc., of education, and (rightly) realizing that education is a practical job, many people concluded (wrongly) that 'practical' should be interpreted along non-intellectualistic lines. The enterprise was construed as analogous to the more down-to-earth arts and crafts, success in which is chiefly a matter of skill, knack and experience; and in which one learns chiefly by trying to do whatever it is, with the help of a professional who can do it already, like an apprentice. Learning to educate, on this view, is like learning to make pots, or be a carpenter, or sail a boat, or handle horses: there is a fairly severe limit to the usefulness of lectures or abstract ratiocination in these enterprises. Not a few people can be found to say that teacher training should really take place in schools, not in separate institutions of higher education: just like any other apprenticeship. But again for fairly obvious reasons, this will not do either. Whatever important mistakes are made by educators, they are not made because of a lack of practical *skill*, in any normal sense of that word. It is not, to put it another way, that bad educators lack *technique*, or have been given the wrong tips, or have somehow not acquired the *knack*. (It matters a lot what words we use here.) The mistakes lie somewhere in the area of, for instance, lack of enthusiasm for one's subject or for communicating it, inability to stay calm (or get angry) when required, a doctrinaire attitude towards discipline, undue tough- or tender-mindedness towards children, uncertainty about one's own worth, and so forth. There are, of course, useful things that are fairly described as skills or techniques – but they do not carry a teacher very far. As with 'theory', we know quite well that a good teacher can get away with using none of the approved techniques, and conversely that knowledge of the techniques will not make a bad teacher even competent, let alone good; and this is because being a good teacher is no more a matter of 'practical skill' (in the sense under discussion) than a matter of 'theory'.

It is perhaps inevitable in a technological, utilitarian and instrumentalist society that these models should dominate our thinking. We construe teaching and educating on the analogy of business: we have to 'make things work', show 'competence', be 'accountable' for 'efficiency'. The trouble is, of course, that it is not clear what *counts* as 'working' in education, any more than, say, in marriage or friendship or religion: so that words like 'competence' and 'efficient' either seem inappropriate or have to be stretched. (Was Socrates an *efficient* teacher? Was Abelard *competent*?) There is in fact a double mistake here. First, the ends are always questionable: what counts as 'working', if we insist on the term, will depend on what one is trying to achieve: and second, what makes things 'work' (in any worthwhile sense) is not reducible to practical skills and techniques, nor to theoretical knowledge. It lies somewhere else, in an area where other terms are appropriate – perhaps 'sanity', 'clarity of mind', 'non-doctrinaire attitudes', 'wisdom', 'insight' and others. Societies prepared even to consider insisting on 'behavioural objectives' are not likely to take kindly to this sort of talk, nor to take seriously the task of making it less vague and more amenable to institutionalization than it must seem from our brief description here.

There are parallels to the kind of corruption spread by these models ('theory' and 'practice'). It is as if one thought that being a good husband or even a good lover was primarily a matter, either of reading up a lot of psychoanalytic theory, or of the practical skills of sexual athleticism: neither in themselves despicable, but clearly omitting the most important area, where we would use terms like 'considerate', 'understanding', 'passionate', 'loyal', etc.: or as if we believed that central to the training of priests were the practical skills of not spilling the communion wine, or not rustling the pages of the Bible too loudly when they read the lesson; or that being a good parent was primarily a matter of mixing 'theory' (from Freud or whoever) with the 'practice' of having enough children to have 'gained the relevant experience'. But it is simply not like that.

It is difficult to spell out in detail just what it is like without the use of examples, of which we will take only one. A teacher's attitude to and understanding of rules, discipline and punishment is on any account important. Improvement here is chiefly a matter of: (a) a proper conceptual grasp of these things, and (b) acquiring the feelings that ought to go along with such a grasp. Doctrinaire attitudes to authority – say, the hatred of any kind of rules or legitimized power-wielders – emerge both in conceptual muddle or misunderstanding and in the rawer feelings of expressed preferences and ideologies: (a) and (b) interconnect. There may of course also be (c) the acquiring of new and sophisticated empirical information above the level of common sense; but the central problems will be the overcoming of prejudice and fantasy, the development of a serious (as opposed to an autistic) attitude to these matters, and a more sophisticated critical, or self-conscious, grasp of the whole area.

We may call the methods here by such names as 'philosophy' (conceptual clarity) and 'psychology' (understanding of feelings) if we like; but it is important, whatever we call them, to avoid two mistakes. First, we must appreciate that many (most? all?) people are, *vis-à-vis* certain areas, in a much worse mental state than can be improved by the immediate application of any intellectual discipline as normally practised. A seminar on corporal punishment I once ran began with one participant saying, 'I don't see the point of discussing this: after all, *who would dream of laying hands on the sacred person of a child*?' What is wrong here was not lack of academic intelligence (or knowledge of 'theory'), nor yet lack of practice (the person was an experienced teacher): it lies rather in the dimension of the sensible as against the doctrinaire, the sane as against the fanatical. If we raise the question of how to make some sort of rational impact on a person of this kind, it is clear that we shall have to consider (though not here) the context and relationships between student and teacher, not only the content. It is no good simply listing the names of various disciplines and shoving them at teachers in what are thought to be suitable doses; almost everything turns on the way in which they are brought to bear. Secondly, however, we must not think that this makes the content of teacher training 'non-intellectual', as if it were simply a matter of 'feeling'. For one (perhaps the most important because the only reliable) way of changing one's feelings is via the use of one's intellect: ultimately there is (in this context) not much point in philosophy, psychology and other related disciplines unless they help us to see certain aspects or parts of life more clearly, and thus enable us to change both our feelings and our behaviour.

Chapter 4

The child within us

There are many ways in which – whether as teachers, or parents, or anyone thinking about education – we may be tempted to go wrong because of our own inner feelings. Unsurprisingly, these feelings stem from our own childhood experiences: it is 'the child within us', one might say, that too often overcomes the rational adult. There is a lot that might be said here, but for our purposes it may be sufficient to describe two basic ways in which we are tempted to go wrong. Both ways stem ultimately from two different postures or attitudes to authority: at least they can be usefully so described.

1. The first involves *identification* with authority. Here the individual (or the society as a whole) sees him or herself as the unquestionable representative of a corpus of truths and values: teachers have the 'right answers', and their job is to pass these on to their pupils so that they end up believing them and acting in accordance with them. Confident in this assumption, the teacher welcomes the power, authority, sanctions and disciplinary measures deemed necessary to put it into practice. The authority may be described or rationalized in different ways: 'Marxist ideology', 'a Christian way of life', 'British (French, etc.) culture and traditions', 'middle-class values' or whatever. This posture is visible, in extreme forms, in totalitarian and authoritarian societies – though of course not confined to them.
2. The second involves *rejection* of authority. Here individuals are in a state of reaction against whatever they take to be current authorities ('the establishment'). Such teachers do not regard their own beliefs and values as having priority over others, or as forming a firm and secure basis for education: they may indeed adopt some kind of relativist position in which the objectivity of truth and values is itself called into question or even denied. They are likely to favour a non-hierarchical ideology, and some kind of egalitarianism (as it were, dismantling

existing authority and dissipating it throughout society), along with certain interpretations of 'democracy' or 'participation': and they are likely to favour 'integration' and object to some practices as 'divisive' or 'élitist'. This posture is visible more often in liberal and pluralistic societies (the UK is a fair example).

It is easy to see how each of these strays from the concept of education. On the one hand, (1) the notion of education – indeed of learning itself – is connected with the logically basic notion of a *rational stance* towards the world. It is this stance that is primary: items claimed as truth or knowledge or worthwhile values derive their validity from that stance, from the primary concept of reasonable procedures, rather than vice versa. 'Right answers' cannot be the starting-point of education, since their rightness (if they are indeed right) can only be a function of the criteria of reason which justify them as right. This is perhaps most obvious in the case of moral education, where it is clear that no first-order set of values – no specific moral *content* – can be taken for granted: for such education we have to rely on initiating pupils into a grasp of the rational procedures which they can use to generate their own values. Objections to indoctrination, or the socialization of pupils into norms and practices that may well be questioned, rest ultimately on this point, as do the legitimate demands under such headings as 'autonomy' and 'critical thinking'. In a word: the only authority an educator can ultimately recognize is the authority of reason itself, not of any particular or partisan ideology. On the other hand, (2) to dismantle or reject authority in general, to fall into any kind of relativism, to react against the whole concept of 'right answers', is equally to stray from education: for the notions of reason, learning, knowledge, truth and hence of education itself are connected to that concept. Rational procedures (if we can get clear about them) do have authority, and educators can and must have authority in so far as they act as representatives of these procedures – for instance, as representatives and teachers of how to think reasonably about the physical world (science), about the past (history) and so on. Further, educators need the practical or social authority necessary to transmit these procedures to their pupils: briefly, the authority and power necessary to enforce whatever discipline is required for education.

Of the two general temptations already mentioned in (1) and (2) above, (1) is a much simpler reaction: the individual simply takes on the mantle of authority passed on by his or her parents (or elders, or whoever represents 'the establishment'). That reaction may be regarded as in some sense the natural state, and the reaction of rejection as more complex and sophisticated, at least at the public or social level. (I do not deny that the psychic roots of rejection lie very deep, as the work of such post-Freudians as Melanie Klein shows.) Again, at a public or social level, increased communications and a widespread surge in the desire for 'liberation' or 'autonomy' – one might say generally, for 'doing one's own thing' – make (1) much more difficult to sustain; to continue the tradition of an authoritarian folk society in the face of potential revolution and a desire for independence is extremely difficult in the modern world. Finally, there is some evidence (though I shall not discuss it here) that those who control and operate education in many societies, particularly in the Western world, favour (2) rather than (1): for instance, that in pluralistic societies many of the most articulate and influential teachers and educators have gone in for the rejection of authority in a fairly big way, favouring relativism, egalitarianism, 'integration' and other ideas that symptomatize that rejection.

These points are of course very briefly stated, and much sociological and psychological enquiry needs to be devoted to them: further, it is of course always true that the opposite reaction (1) is permanently available and will to some extent occur by a swing of the pendulum or even concurrently. Thus the dissatisfaction with 'liberal' or 'wishy-washy' religious and moral education may generate a desire to have one's children educated in much more authoritarian regimes, perhaps based on fundamentalist religious principles or some other hard-line ideology. This seems now to be occurring in many parts of the world. The motives here are, again, not always complex: a desire for security at all costs, a clear and hard line, a fear of some sort of schizoid split (both in society and in the individual psyche) which can only be staved off by a *simpliste* and uncritical acceptance of a straightforward ideology, a 'faith to live by', 'law and order', 'the preservation of standards and traditions' – all these are fairly familiar to us, and have been tolerably well documented, sometimes under headings like 'the authoritarian personality'. Reaction (2) is more complex, and deserves our more immediate attention.

The most useful procedure is to try to pin down what we often seem to be *frightened* of, what we hate, or what (as it were) raises our hackles. Amongst these seem to be:

1. The idea of segregating or differentiating between people.
2. The exercise of any kind of judgement, punishment or domination.
3. Impersonal authority.
4. Objectivity (of values, knowledge, concepts).
5. Competition or conflict.

Some of these, again, are perhaps not discrete. Thus it seems likely that the fear of differentiation in (1), and perhaps also of objectivity in (4), are generated by the fear of domination in (2): the thought – conscious or unconscious – is perhaps something like 'We must not differentiate, otherwise we establish a hierarchy in which those at the bottom of the pile suffer'. (This thought seems to me very clearly to lie at the root of much thinking in the areas of race and gender.) Similarly, the idea of objectivity suggests potential domination by those who are the repositories of supposed objective values. (Perhaps the commonest speech-form used by those alarmed by this is 'Who are *you* (we) to impose *your* (our) values on ...?' – followed by some supposedly underprivileged group.) It is less threatening to adopt some kind of relativism, so that at least the thoughts and feelings and practices of individuals are not challenged or crushed by any objective standards.

Further illustration of these reactions (though desirable in a fuller work) is not in place here: they lead us, pretty quickly and obviously, to the position of the young child. A young child's position is essentially power-less: that is the inevitable price s/he pays for being raised from infancy – being looked after, fed, taught and (of course) told how to behave. Children are in effect under a parental mandate, in which their freedom and power are abrogated. Of course they feel ambivalent about this: on the one hand, they want the security which the mandate gives them (psycho-logical as well as material security), but on the other they resent parental domination. Clearly, any development of a potentially rational creature from birth to adulthood faces this general problem, and would face it in any family or set of social conditions. Ideally, the problem is solved (with more or less difficulty) by a mixture of affection, love, concern, sharing, tender-ness and care on the one hand, and the application of concepts like discipline, rules, punishment, obedience, and the reality pressures of other people's rights and demands of the external world on the other.

All that is (I hope) common ground, constantly retrodden in almost all books on child-rearing or child psychology. But because children are striving towards adulthood, that part of their minds and thoughts which fears, resents and hates adult power is apt to be uppermost (and hence finds more frequent expression than the need for security and limits which they also feel). They do not want (1) to be differentiated as children, or (2) to be judged and dominated: they prefer to do what they are told only if and when they feel warm enough to adults as individual people, not imperso-nally (3). They reject the alleged objectivity of adult values (4), but at the same time do not wish to be the losers (as they almost certainly will be) in any competition or conflict (5).

A good deal of this is to do with the fear of domination or of one's own aggression; but some of it is also to do with separation anxiety. Children inevitably live in a world which sometimes seems a world of isolation and slavery; they are alone, powerless, surrounded by adults larger and better equipped, where their only allies are other children, the peer group. (Hence, unsurprisingly, the immense power of the peer group – whether in the form of street gangs or any other – in modern liberal society: they represent the only defence against the powerful adult.) Impersonal adult authority – the police, for instance – is particularly intolerable because the authority is here divorced from the idea of adults as also caring and sharing parents: the child is brought up sharply against impersonal notions like rules and their attached penalties.

This is essentially a paranoid position: and it has, I think, to be accepted that all children are inevitably paranoid. This is not a cheap pseudo-psychiatric jibe, but a simple recognition of an inevitable psychological posture adopted by the small and weak in the face of what is, indeed, virtually total domination by the adult. For the children, of course, are not able to appreciate the necessities of any form of child-rearing, the necessity of adult power; and even – which is by no means always and everywhere the case – when the adults use their mandated power for the child's benefit, the *feelings* of the child may remain hostile, suspicious and fearful, even if the child is capable of some intellectual grasp of the necessary mandate. As I have said, successful child-rearing gradually weans the child from the paranoid position, by sharing and discipline; but even the best upbringing leaves many of these feelings untouched in the unconscious mind.

It is easy to see how the business of being an educator – a parent or a teacher – regenerates one's own paranoid feelings by reactivating one's own childhood position. Interestingly, those who are most vehement in expressing some of the ideas and feelings listed above have not, in fact, always grown up in families or schools where the mandate was much abused. They are not the offspring of some tyrannical Victorian paterfamilias, but have often grown up in extremely liberal circumstances. It is the *idea* (again, often unconscious) of the highly punitive adult rather than the real-life existence of such an adult that seems to count: and that idea becomes more ferocious and threatening when adults resign their authority and try to behave more like children themselves. For the child is fully aware (more than the adult) that there is virtually infinite power on the adult side: and if the adult seems to deny or conceal this by behaving with too much liberality and not enough authority, the child naturally supposes that there is, as it were, another more powerful and threatening figure behind the real one. (There is a useful parallel here with what Tacitus says in his *Annals* about the Roman emperors: the bad ones were bad, and the apparently benevolent and good ones must somehow have been concealing their badness under a cloak of liberality, thus adding hypocrisy to their other vices – a very clear example of an unfalsifiable paranoid outlook.)

Adults who abdicate from their positions of authority, under the influence of the reactivated paranoid child within themselves, are of course particularly frightened by the use of what one may term *naked power*, because the possibility of deploying such power brings their problems to a head. It is here that the compulsive quality of their fears becomes most apparent: for it is one thing to encourage, cajole, support or even bribe children into obedience, but quite another to say something like 'Look, you have got to do this, and without caring whether you like or respect me as a person I am going to make life sufficiently unpleasant for you to make sure that you do actually do it'. Only adults who feel themselves metaphysically backed by God, or the Party, or some other legitimating agency who will give them the required nerve and self-confidence, can easily take such a line: and, in contemporary liberal and pluralist societies, not many such adults are left – at least, in the educational world. It is, of course, an unpleasant line to have to take: yet any parents who (for instance) need to stop, say, their son bullying a little sister, or any honest teacher who needs to make absolutely sure that the weak pupils are not done down by the strong in school, knows perfectly well that such a line has sometimes to be taken. Yet, for many people, this is the sticking-point; to apply straightforward fear as a motive – particularly fear of overt forms of power, such as corporal punishment – seems to them morally intolerable and (for themselves) psychologically out of the question.

We may here usefully compare professional pacifists; and certainly it is not only with children that this compulsion is evident. In the politics of most liberal societies, certain kinds of action are, as they say, just 'not acceptable'. The kinds of force, for instance, that might be required to crush terrorism, or even football hooliganism, seem in themselves intolerable: we prefer, it seems, to allow the weak to be bullied and killed rather than use such ferocious methods. This is a kind of moral absolutism which, whatever may be said for it at the philosophical level, nevertheless clearly stems from a deep fear of power and violence. It is of course an empirical question what forms of power are necessary to deploy in order to get rid of what sorts of social disorder, but one has some sympathy with an old lady whose arm was broken by football hooligans; when told that much research was being done on the social causes of such hooliganism: she said 'What they ought to do research on is why the authorities don't stop it'.

The deployment of violence, indeed of any form of power, is no doubt something which any civilized person must consider seriously; but it is a fantasy to suppose that we can shield children from it. Children experience, and have to come to terms with, much more profound and naked fear than anything which adults normally admit to the conscious mind. Their fear of actual, real-life adult power and punishment is by no means the worst of their fears: indeed the deployment of such power may come as a kind of relief. The super-ego (if I may use this terminology) is not and could not be built up in children by any amount of kindness, affection or rational explanation alone: it is inevitably based on the fear of some kind of retribution. We do children no kindness if we behave as if that were not so: what we can do is to give that retribution some sort of manageable shape and some connection with the real world, so that it can develop into a respectable adult conscience.

The paranoid fear of violence and domination would be less destructive in educational social practice if it were confined merely to the compulsive taboo on overt or dramatic forms of force: for instance, on forms such as torture, or hanging or severe corporal punishment. Unfortunately the fear lies so deep, and is so well defended in the conscious mind by various forms of rationalization ('violence breeds violence', 'a caring attitude', and so on), that it extends to the whole business of interaction between those in authority and their clients. It is now more or less standard practice in some educational circles that teachers are encouraged not to confront disruptive or disobedient pupils, but rather to 'defuse' potential conflict by some form of evasive action – smoothing things over, cajolery, humour, or whatever. The pupil challenges the teacher's authority, but the challenge is evaded rather than met head on. Given that teachers have in fact little real power to make their authority stick (since the paranoia is institutionalized in the educational system, which in liberal societies does not trust teachers with enough power), teachers can hardly be blamed for using such methods: they have often to act as advisers or missionaries rather than as authorities, and keep some semblance of order in any way they can. But the psychological results are clearly corrupting: for the pupil is treated not as a person in a world where there are rules and other people with their own interests, but rather as a 'case' who (one is tempted to say, which) has to be 'handled'. The effect is not to educate, but to avoid trouble at all costs: to keep the temperature down. Yet at some point, and backed by some clear deployment of authority together with whatever force, pressure or sanctions are needed to make the authority stick, any educator must bring it home to pupils that there are certain limits beyond which they are not allowed to go – if necessary, forcibly prevented from going. In this way an essential feature in the development towards adulthood is blurred: the child is not even allowed to face the necessary conflict and hence not allowed to make a psychological adjustment towards reality. The whole concept of authority, and also of discipline (which is essentially obedience to legitimate authority), is abandoned in favour of a desperate and doomed attempt to preserve some kind of order without infringing the taboos against fear and force.

If we now raise the question of how we may hope to cure or educate ourselves out of this paranoid position, it is above all important to avoid the equal and opposite error of identification with some (any) authority which seems to offer hope by 'taking a firm line', 'standing for solid values', or whatever. This move tends to occur in history with boring regularity. An authority exists and is respected: later it is undermined (often for good reasons, since many authorities are irrational and unjust): there follows a period of anomie, chaos or uncertainty; another authority is then produced and the cycle starts again. (Many would say that something like this has been happening in the recent history of British politics.) It is as if the child within us were unable to grasp the concept of rational authority, being capable only either of swallowing some personal or charismatic authority hook, line and sinker, or else of retreating to some sort of egalitarian, relativistic and in general anti-authority position: either we must identify with some specific and substantive set of 'solid values', a partisan moral or political or religious line, or else each of us can do what he likes according to his fancy. That apparent dilemma, which has inhibited the advance of any serious moral (or political or religious) education, is now as powerful as it has always been, despite its intellectual absurdity; and it is, obviously enough, the direct result of retaining the ways in which the world appears to us as young children – either we blindly obey the powerful adults, or we just do what we feel like.

We escape from this, of course, as with any other kind of mental illness, only by first of all recognizing it; but the chief difficulty that has to be faced is the almost total lack of any public context or arena which encourages such recognition. In educational circles much of what passes as 'theory', or is considered as supposedly rational and objective exploration of various educational issues and ideologies, tends to be not much more than the acting out of particular ideologies that merely echo either the paranoid position described earlier or the reactive identification with some (any) authority at all costs – perhaps some severe or fundamentalist kind of religion, for instance. As with arguments about religion, nearly all the crucial moves have already been made unconsciously before the arguments start: and often what is supposed to be free and frank rational discussion turns out to be a pietistic exercise in which the faithful reinforce their own fantasies.

On any account – and, as I need to stress here, quite independently of whether my own descriptions are at all accurate – education is an extremely difficult area: not merely 'controversial', but liable to the sort of unconscious pressures we have been talking about. The mere recognition of this in principle (without specific diagnoses) should lead to establishing contexts and methods in which we can hope to fight our way out of fantasy. It is in fact fairly plain what such contexts and methods would look like: suffice it to say here that they must involve the close analysis of concepts and feelings in small group discussion. Such a context is an attempt to introduce (or reintroduce) both staff and students to something that ought to have happened (or, rarely, has happened) to the young child in a well-ordered and loving family. In such a family, the children come to grasp the idea and practices of rational discussion – a very sophisticated notion to which all educators need to pay far more attention than they usually do. The children learn to wean themselves from the merely autistic expression of their own feelings (or the equally autistic fear of saying anything at all), and to take part in a kind of public game with rules and procedures of its own. They have to submit themselves to criticism, not mind too much about making a fool of themselves, attend to the meanings of the words they use, make some respectable connection between what they *feel* and what can truthfully or sensibly be *said*, exercise tact and tolerance towards others, not become too angry, not take criticism personally, stick to the point, face the facts, keep the rules of logic, and so forth. This (rag-bag and fragmentary) list of procedures and abilities carries one overall message with it: roughly, that when interacting with other people (not just in discussion but in life generally) *one's own particular views, feelings and 'commitments' must take second place to the overall procedures of reason*: even when – *particularly* when – one's feelings are especially passionate.

This is of course a very hard lesson to learn. Its importance is both obvious and wide-ranging: for one thing, the whole business of interpersonal morality (of which interpersonal discussion is merely one context) rests on the acceptance of some principle of universalizability (see Hare, 1981) – roughly, that there is nothing special about one's own desires (including one's own ideals). We constantly try to evade it, both at the theoretical and the practical level: we want to be able to think that some views (those we particularly hate or are frightened of) are intolerable, beyond the pale, clearly absurd. At the same time we do not want to be the ones whose views are thus censured: so we pay some kind of lip-service to universalizability without always practising it. (The test of a genuine belief in various forms of universalizability – tolerance, for instance – is that it should sometimes cost us an effort: that it should sometimes *hurt*.)

The (again obvious but commonly neglected) psychological point is that we are unlikely to learn this lesson unless our learning is rewarded. In the family, the child learns to play this game with loving parents: the reward is not so much extrinsic, but comes from the child's pleasure in sharing something that the parents have to offer, wanting to imitate them and enjoy what they enjoy. There is a close parallel here with the sharing of food and drink, and of other mutual pleasures less sophisticated than discussion; indeed it is arguable that more primitive forms of sharing are a necessary step towards the more sophisticated. This must mean that those leading group discussion have much more psychological work to do than make an hour or two's space for seminars: they have somehow to interact and share with the group sufficiently to generate something like the trust and security of family discussion. That has obvious implications for the structure, timing and organization of such groups: implications that educational institutions need to take much more seriously.

Part II

Teaching and learning

Chapter 5

The curriculum

I

The most striking, and alarming, thing about the curriculum (or 'curricular theory', whatever that may be) is that debates and discussions never seem to get anywhere. I do not mean, of course, that decisions and policies are not arrived at and (sometimes) implemented; I mean that there seems to be no publicly and rationally agreed *advance in knowledge*. We are not able to build on established propositions, able to say 'Well, at least we now know that such-and-such pupils ought – for overwhelmingly and demonstrably good reasons – to learn such-and-such, taught in such-and-such a way: so now let us try to take things further'. Arguments continue about not only the methods of teaching various subjects, but also about their value: indeed even about the nature of each subject and what is to count as a 'subject'. Fashions, climates of opinion and various political (in a broad sense of that word) pressures come and go, and this or that 'consensus' may prevail at different times: but the notion of rational agreement seems hard to realize in practice, for various reasons:

1. Certainly one important (perhaps the most important) reason for this is that we cannot avoid making judgements of value in this area, and that educators and administrators tend to fight shy of making such judgements: or more precisely, since the actual making of them is inevitable, tend not to see the process of forming and defending value judgements as a potentially rational process, subject to certain rules and procedures and types of expertise. The business of (a) expressing one's own values or preferences, and of (b) getting some kind of consensus, by political negotiation, about values, important though these may be, are quite different from (c) the process of working out, by debate and the application of reason, what values are actually *right*. Indeed, in a climate of relativism and ideology, many people talk as if (c) were in

principle impossible or improper; and that, of course, makes any rational progress impossible.

2. A second difficulty, easy to underrate, is that for various reasons the concept marked by 'curriculum' itself is not properly understood or agreed. I have argued elsewhere (Wilson, 1977) that in normal usage – i.e. when not distorted by educationalists and others – the term refers to the teaching and learning of various *subjects* in some fairly coherent and structured way: it is close to the concept of a syllabus, and does not include just *any* learning (let alone anything that happens in a school). Pupils may learn from being made to take cold baths, or from being bullied in the playground or spoken to kindly by teachers in the corridor; but it would be odd to say that these things were part of a *curriculum*. The point here has nothing to do with linguistic purity; it is that we desperately need clear and well-separated categories under which to assess school life, and hence have to place clear demarcations on each category. We need to distinguish 'curriculum' from (say) 'pastoral care', 'school ethos' and other possible categories. Over-inflating the term will make nothing clearer. (Thus it is a real and important question of how far moral education, for instance, is a *curricular* matter: given a reasonably clear demarcation of 'curriculum', as above, we can at least begin to see what aspects of moral education can profitably be taught as a subject, and what aspects are better done under some other heading. Without the distinction we cannot even approach the question sensibly.)

3. A third difficulty, which is connected with the two above, is that we tend to be so anxious about certain other features of the curriculum that we never give ourselves a chance to consider the worth of this or that *content*. We are anxious to say, perhaps, that subjects in the curriculum should be 'integrated', that there should be no improper 'barriers': or that children should not be taught just 'facts' but also 'skills' or 'atti-tudes' ('caring', 'concern', 'personal relationships', and so on): or that it should not be unduly 'middle-class', or 'irrelevant' to pupils' daily lives: or whatever. Such matters, however important, do nothing to settle what must surely be the initial question about any curriculum: that is, *what is worth teaching and learning*, and to what pupils. It is a point of such importance that nearly all *other* decisions – decisions about how to teach it, or how often, or whether this or that subject should be compulsory, or whether this or that sort of pupil will benefit from it – can only be made later. For the methods and practices of teaching/learning X are bound to be, in large part, a function of what X is and what we take to be important about X.

4. Finally (at this level of practicality), there is the difficulty that we tend to take existing subject titles for granted. We have, in effect, just a set of *words* – 'classics', 'French', 'science', 'RE' and so forth – with a set of (constantly changing) practices attached to them. These titles and practices have grown up for a wide variety of reasons: some practical

(science becomes more important to a society, so finds a place in the curriculum), some ideological (religious believers make a place for RE): in general, the development of the curriculum in the history of any educational system has been uncritical and *ad hoc*. But we too often take for granted that these titles represent the kind of categorization or taxonomy that we want: we assume that they divide up possible curricular content in the best way. Hence most public documents simply juggle these titles around, inserting 'a modern language', 'some basic science', 'English' and others apparently on the assumption that we already have the goods on sale properly sorted out into various departments, and need only make a judicious selection. But it is quite clear that we cannot assume this, if only because what the titles in fact stand for changes, often quite dramatically, over time: thus 'classics' now stands for a very different set of practices in most schools than the ones it used to stand for a century ago. Briefly, we do not know either just what the titles are titles *of*, or whether they are the titles we need.

II

When we reach a proper appreciation of these initial difficulties – and I am bound to say that nearly all curricular discussion and change fails to reach it – we face squarely what must be the first real problem, at which I have hinted above: that is, *how* are we to categorize or taxonomize the items? It is important to realize in advance that many different taxonomies are possible, and quite a few may be important to us. Whether a subject is easy or difficult, whether it is cheap or expensive to teach, whether we have or lack teachers trained to teach it, whether it is 'relevant to the modern world', whether it is likely to appeal only to certain categories of pupils, whether it represents a *sui generis* form of thought – all these are respectable candidates, and there are plenty of others. Unsurprisingly philosophers (notably Hirst: the clearest exposition is in Hirst and Peters, 1970) have opted for the last criterion of differentiation: that is, for dividing items of knowledge up into *logically* different categories. Even the attempt to do this is very valuable for anyone planning a curriculum, if only because it makes us think harder about just what differences in method or style of thinking do actually exist in various subjects. (The difference between asking why planets behave in certain ways and asking why people behave is clearly central to anyone thinking about science, history, psychology and other subjects: the 'why' has a different sense in either case, and a whole different methodology and approach go along with this.) But why should these logical differences be, in some stronger sense, *important*? To use a parallel: suppose we were asking what games we wanted to initiate our pupils into, the *logical* differences between games (in terms of types of rules, perhaps) might not be all that significant. Certainly other criteria would be relevant (does such-and-such a game foster too much competition, is it cheap enough, can it only be played by intellectuals, and above all *is it a good game?*).

This last thought – is it a good game? – brings us back, inevitably and rightly, to the central question of what knowledge or experience we take as worth while or valuable in general; and I want to advance the suggestion that we should attempt some sort of approach to this question *before* saddling ourselves with *any* taxonomy – or rather, that making some progress with the question is the best way into seeing what taxonomy we need. I am not aware that philosophers (or modern philosophers at least) have been of much service to curricular theorists in this matter. Part of the trouble, I think, is that not many such philosophers adopt and argue for any clear set of values: they tend, like the rest of us, to convey at least the appearance of assuming that *all* the items and categories are of equal importance, and hence of being reduced to the (for some, attractively 'liberal') position of suggesting only that pupils be given a taste of each category. Contrast this, just for the sake of illustration, with the views of a strong religious believer who might hold that knowledge of salvation was the only really important thing, other items being mere amusements; or of a strong revolutionary Marxist who might hold that a certain kind of political education was so vital that anything else was not much more than a waste of time. As so often, liberals tend to behave as if they not only thought (rightly) that education should not be founded on some ultimately unjustified and arbitrary ideology, but also thought (wrongly) that no serious position about the comparative values of this or that subject could be put forward: thus falling into a sort of supermarket or shop-window view of the curriculum, which may keep everyone comparatively happy (since no one's views are down-graded) but fails to tackle the question seriously at all.

III

In this position it is very important to *go slowly* and not to rush into setting up the 'right answers'. One thing that can be done, as I have explained elsewhere (Wilson, 1979), is to distinguish the *types of argument* that might be brought forward on behalf of this or that curricular item; and it is not too hard to distinguish between

1. items desirable not *per se* but for some extrinsic ('utilitarian') purpose and
2. items desirable 'for their own sake': a tendentious phrase, but suggesting that their value does not depend on the particular necessities of, say, Britain in the 1990s.

Thus, depending largely on local conditions, it may be of great importance (1) to teach pupils how to fly Spitfires, get on well with microchips or cars, work certain kinds of machines, and so forth – things for which the question 'What's the use of ...?' would be appropriate. On the other hand (2), a defence of classical music, chess, art, literature and other such things would look quite different: we should try to show that these things were important to *people as such*, not to individuals who had to survive and prosper under a particular set of economic or social conditions.

This (rather obvious but little used) distinction would, in fact, carry us quite a long way. Instead of just thinking, rather vaguely, that 'science' or 'French' was 'important', we should have to state more precisely (1) what practical *use* it was in, say, Britain over the next few decades, and (2) what intrinsic value or worthwhileness it had – what there was 'in it' in its own right. We should also come to see that *educators* were not the right people to determine (1): presumably governments or employers or some such people were better placed to tell us about what pupils needed to learn in point of social or economic viability: but that (2) might well be left to educators and academics, whose speciality it is to explore and understand the intrinsic merits of certain subjects, together with the ways in which they can best be passed on to pupils. Again, we should also see that almost every subject-title had to be approached from both angles, and might often split up into two: for instance, 'English' as construed (1) merely as involving certain facts or skills necessary for social viability would be, in effect, a different subject from 'English' as (2) some sort of worthwhile possession or enterprise for any person anywhere (even on a desert island). So too, clearly enough, with 'maths': a maths course designed for (1) would look very different from one designed for (2) – though, of course, we should rejoice in any overlap.

That represents some advance in our grasp of different *types* of justification: and also shows just how much easier it has been for us to concentrate on (1) rather than (2). We have some idea, or think we have, about what is immediately and practically useful or important to today's pupils; a less clear notion of what is important to any person, or why it is. Hence the over-playing of notions marked by 'practical', 'relevant' and 'useful'. We may even think that pupils themselves, who do indeed often ask 'What's the *use* of ...?', favour (1) as against (2): only to remember, if we do remember, that pupils in practice favour such activities as football, pop music and sex, none of which are obviously 'useful' – just as fairy-tales and the writings of Tolkien are, in one sense, much more 'outside the everyday experience' of young people, yet appeal to them as much or more than modern novels about contemporary housing estates.

The trouble with (1) is not, of course, that it may not be important. Nobody thinks that pupils should not be employable, or should not have the skills which alone may enable their country to earn its economic living, or should be ignorant of facts which any individual or citizen in a particular society ought to know. The trouble is that (1) is a *fragile* category; no sooner do we insist on a particular skill than improved technology (calculators) or changed circumstances make it obsolete. (Increased automation and high unemployment represent just one illustration of this.) We need, certainly, a much more well thought out and precisely itemized list of what we want to put into (1); and, if the items really are essential, to teach them as hard as we can. Some items, like elementary reading and writing and computation, may be non-controversial: others may change over time, and rightly if circumstances change. All that is, in principle, clear enough and not hard to negotiate. But it leaves us with category (2), which is not only important in itself (since people are human beings as well as citizens of a particular society), but likely to become more important in the future.

IV

So far as category (2) is concerned – what is important *for people as such* to learn – we have to take our courage in both hands and produce a well-reasoned view of the human condition: what used to be called a 'doctrine of man'. This is not the place to advance such a view in any adequately defended form; but there is one general question which must immediately present itself to anyone considering the matter. Given candidates which are not 'useful' in any obvious sense – art, music, literature, philosophy, and indeed those aspects of 'useful' subjects like science and mathematics which are desirable for non-utilitarian reasons – are we to view them as (a) just *fun* ('enriching', 'cultural', etc.), or (b) as actually *needed* by human beings in some more serious sense? To put the point briefly: either Mozart operas, Shakespeare, the history of the Renaissance and so on are just pastimes for intellectuals (into which we might hope to initiate some pupils, perhaps on the grounds that they may come to find more pleasure in Beethoven than in beer), or else they *matter*.

We commonly act and talk as if (a) were true: again, I suspect, because of our fear of imposing any ideology on our fellows, or making them feel guilty if they have not read Tolstoy, or down-grading pupils who may never be able to engage in such highbrow activities. But we are not here concerned with high and low brows: again, either music (art, literature, etc.) is just for fun, or else it is *needed* – at whatever level or in whatever form different pupils may best take it up. In fact, most people who have any genuine love or appreciation of these things, at any level, believe (b) rather than (a): they regard them as in some way integral to their lives, not just sideline amusements; somehow instructive or educational or anyway important to them as people, not just for the pleasure they give but for the lessons they teach and the way in which they shape the fabric of their lives. The difficulty is to defend (b) above the level of mere rhetoric (talk of 'culture' or 'civilization'). We have to ask *why* they matter. And this question presents itself not only for the kind of content items I have mentioned, but also for the items which represent the development of particular skills or abilities or attitudes: we need to ask in each case 'Why do "social skills", or learning to make friends, or caring for other people, or reading a novel intelligently, matter to any person?'

Whether we opt for (a) or (b) will depend, I think, on whether we see the human condition (a) primarily as *all right*, afflicted indeed by certain difficulties but difficulties that are not all that hard in principle to remove (perhaps by 'changing society'); or (b) as in some way deeply and obscurely difficult, afflicted by original sin, or *mauvaise foi*, or neurosis, or something of that kind. If (a), then these curricular items will be, at best, just a sort of cultural top-dressing which it is nice (not essential) for men to possess: if (b), they will appear as essential bits of equipment for the attainment of happiness or any sort of worthwhile life; to put it dramatically, for salvation. My guess is that the more any serious person (with or without the benefit of religion, or philosophy, or Greek or Shakespearean tragedy, or Freud) reflects on this matter, the more he or she is likely to be driven towards (b); and there are, I believe, irrefutable arguments why (b) must be right – briefly, arguments to do with the inevitable difficulties of developing an ego or rational self in early childhood.

It is more important that we face these questions clearly than that I or any other philosopher should persuade educators of this or that answer; but in so far as curriculum-makers would agree with the general trend of what I have said, we can see some hope of progress. Human beings and the human condition being what they are (and of course they need much more description, in literary as well as philosophical terms), it would be possible to see *how* various subjects or other items bear on them – some perhaps more directly than others. We might come to regard certain things (good candidates might include the use of language, the ability to understand and love other human beings) as *central* to being a person, other things as more peripheral or optional. Thus – to stick my neck out – it seems to me that being able to communicate and form personal relationships, and to enjoy doing some job of work for its own sake, are central in a way in which knowing about, say, the behaviour of moths or differential equations is not central, important though these may be for utilitarian reasons; and I think this could be argued for, rather than just stated as preferred ideology. Scientists can make machines for me and cure my body – both very important: but I can only talk to, love and relate to, forgive, enjoy or appreciate people and things for myself. (That is not to down-grade science or other subjects; just to reclassify them.) The arts are important because they shed light (not just pleasure) on people: to read Tolstoy's *Anna Karenina* is to understand self-deception, to which we are all prone, more fully. Is mathematical argument just a useful tool for science, or is it (as Plato thought) something which all men need to practise if their thinking is to be really precise? That sort of question, at least, is the kind we need to raise.

V

It will be clear that we have a long way to go; in particular, that we need much more insight into the intrinsic worth of subjects, something on which little philosophical or other work has been done. Rather than some all-embracing 'curricular theory', we need to understand just what would be lost if a magician were to excise (for instance) a knowledge of French, or poetry or biology from our minds. Only people 'on the inside' of these subjects can help us here; learning from them, we can perhaps slowly come to see different kinds and degrees of importance, and produce not a theory but an order of priorities.

Then – but only then – we should have to take into account a great many other factors, which I have not been concerned with here: for instance, how far pupils should be allowed to specialize in one or another item, how far we can trust pupils' judgement (as against that of educators) in choosing items for themselves, what items can reasonably be made compulsory, what sorts of pupils are suited to what items, and how in fact the items can be best taught. Arguments about these issues, as I hinted earlier, are bound to be premature until we have made more progress (for instance, the notion of 'specialization' is context-dependent or relative, in that it assumes a range of items already given; but we have not established any such range critically).

Finally, the fact that any curricular set-up must (at least for the foreseeable future) be provisional and uncertain strongly suggests that we must educate pupils *directly* in this very topic: that is, in the understanding and discussion of what sorts of things might be important for them to learn. That this is not hopelessly 'abstract' or 'philosophical' is suggested by the successfully taught paper in the international baccalaureate ('theory of knowledge') in which pupils are encouraged to step outside their particular subjects and specialisms, and consider more broadly just what kinds of learning and understanding there are, and what might be said for and against going in for them. This kind of discussion is not, in my judgement, outside the range of (as it is certainly not outside the interest of) pupils of quite average or mediocre ability. One cannot of course get to see what there is in a particular subject in advance of studying it; but that should not inhibit an ongoing discussion on these lines, in which pupils as well as educators should join. The curricular theory of the next generation might be much improved as a result.

Chapter 6

Teaching a subject

A lot of teachers think something like this:

> My subject is mathematics (or English, or geography, or whatever).
> Certainly, there's a lot of argument about how to teach mathematics –
> whether children should be taught to recite the multiplication tables,
> whether we should introduce them to other systems besides the decimal
> system, and so on. But at least I know what mathematics is: after all, I've
> spent a long time learning it myself. And at least I know what it is to
> teach mathematics, even if I'm not sure what the best methods are: after
> all, I've spent a long time teaching it. So isn't it silly to ask general
> questions about subjects, since we know the answers already?

But if we think a bit harder, we may not feel quite as sure of ourselves. With
mathematics and some other subjects (we shall come back to these later) it
seems reasonable to say that we do know at least what the subjects are. But
do we know this with subjects called, say, 'RE' or 'social studies', or
perhaps even 'English'? We may not feel as sure of the content of these
subjects. We may want to ask, 'Just what are we supposed to be doing or
trying to do under these headings? Just what is it to teach RE or social
studies?' And it is important – perhaps also rather alarming – that we are
not entirely clear about the answer. For how can we teach these subjects
well, or indeed at all, if we do not first know what they are?

If we are to get any further with this question, we have to be clear that
we are not asking two other questions. Suppose I am fairly confident that I
know what mathematics is, what it is to teach mathematics. Then I can go
on to ask about the best methods of teaching it (and discuss whether to
make young children learn their tables, etc.), and about the point or aims of
teaching it. (How useful is it in the modern world? Does it improve
children's thinking generally?) These two questions are different, of

course, but they are both also quite different from the issue of what it is to teach X.

It is important to see that we have to start with this issue, for how can we sensibly discuss the best methods of teaching something or the general point of teaching it if we do not know what it is? Suppose we thought about going on a course about the aims and methods of teaching squiggleology. Unless we were pretty clear about what squiggleology was, about what content was covered by the word, we would not know how to start talking about how to teach it or about what point there was in teaching it. Now we are a bit clearer about what some subjects (like mathematics) are than about what squiggleology is, but not always much clearer, although some-times we think we are. A lot of talk about the 'aims and methods of teaching X' (say, English or history, or perhaps even mathematics) may be muddled or a waste of time just because we are not, in fact, as clear about what X is as we like to think.

To put this another way: in a conference about, say, 'teaching English' or 'teaching classics', different people may have quite different ideas about what 'English' or 'classics' is. To one person, perhaps, 'English' means lots of grammar and parsing and neatly written exercises and so on: to another, it means impromptu drama and reading some 'socially relevant' novels with the pupils. Similarly, one person's idea of 'classics' may be learning irregular verbs and construing Caesar; another's may be to give the pupils some idea of what the Greeks and Romans were like, to take them on visits to Roman buildings and so on. Unless we reach some agreement about what we mean by 'English' or 'classics', any discussion on the 'aims and methods' of teaching them will be at cross-purposes.

We all need to hang on to this point tightly because otherwise we are very apt to go off the rails in a certain way. Suppose I am paid to teach music, and I find myself working in a society (perhaps a Communist country) where people are very politically minded. They tell me I should not introduce the children to Beethoven 'because he was a middle-class bourgeois', or that it is wrong for pupils to like Strauss 'because he supported the Nazis'. Now, if I am not careful, I may find myself arguing politics with the authorities. I might say, 'There is nothing wrong with being middle class' or 'Anyone might have made the same mistake as Strauss', or something like that. But what I ought to say is,

> My job is to teach music, not politics: teaching music doesn't have anything to do with politics. It doesn't matter, for anyone interested in music, what Beethoven's or Strauss's political views were. If their political or social views really do help us to understand and appreciate their music, they might be worth mentioning, but otherwise not.

Most of us would probably think that in such cases politics or other marginal considerations are *obviously* irrelevant. But now consider 'teach-ing English'. Suppose the people around me are very keen that children should learn to love their neighbours, or be good citizens or get on well with their friends. They may want me to gear my English teaching to these aims and may put pressure on me to make the pupils read certain books (the ones they think will increase the pupils' 'concern' or 'citizenship') and not others. This is just like the music and politics case, even though here we may have more sympathy with the aims. What we ought to say is,

> No doubt your aims – loving one's neighbour and so on – are very desirable, but that isn't part of what we mean by 'teaching English'. My English teaching may or may not make better or more loving citizens. It may also make the children happier or less happy, more or less able to 'think critically' or 'be creative'. It may have all sorts of 'spin-offs'. But these don't count as part of *what it is to teach English*. Some of them may perhaps count as part of what is meant by, say, 'moral education' or 'civics' but not 'English'.

What happens here is that we get carried away by some external aim, some kind of benefit we want to bestow on our pupils. Perhaps we want them to have the right kind of politics or morality, or not to be indoctrinated with 'middle-class values', or to be happy and socially confident, or 'creative', or 'critical' or 'autonomous'. We call these 'external' aims because (however desirable they may be) they do not count as aims inside the subject. Another example: it may be true, in general, that learning history makes people less prejudiced about other people and races and that it gives them more insight into 'current affairs' – and no doubt these are desirable outcomes. But 'learning history' does not *mean* becoming less prejudiced or better at 'current affairs', as is obvious from the fact that there are people who are good at history or know a lot of history but are still prejudiced and ignorant about all sorts of things. The 'internal' aims of learning history – what counts as 'learning history' – have no necessary connection with the 'external' aim.

It is no good being carried away like this, however important the 'external' aims are. For although we may indeed say things like, 'Teaching history (English etc.) is important because it makes pupils into better citizens and happier people, and this is a crying need, so let's get on with it', we cannot easily know whether this is true; not because we have not done enough research into whether historians make better citizens, but because we have not a clear idea of what 'teaching history' is, so how can we say whether it makes better citizens or not? It is like saying, 'Teaching squiggleology makes happier pupils': it would be no good replying 'Yes, it does' or 'No, it doesn't' – we should have to start by getting clear what squiggleology was.

The only way out of this is a way that we do not think anyone, on reflection, would actually want to take: that is to get rid of the whole idea of 'subjects' altogether. But we can see the temptation. We may think that the child's happiness, or politics, or self-confidence is so important that we should not waste our time on school subjects, and start calling these 'academic' or 'unreal' or 'irrelevant'. So we abolish all subject titles like 'mathematics', 'English', 'history', 'French', and so on (or perhaps we keep one or two extremely vague ones, like 'the environment' or 'society'), and then we find it hard even to ask (let alone answer) questions about what it is to teach any subject.

There are various reasons why this way out is not possible, but it is important first to see that the reason is not that the 'external' aims might be thought unimportant. We are not saying, 'It doesn't matter whether children are happy, "creative", "aware", etc.: they must be made to get on with serious academic work'. The reasons lie deeper. If we are going to do anything we could seriously call educating children (rather than just being nice to them), we will be concerned that they should have some kind of knowledge, or abilities, or skills, or types of competence. But – this is the point – we cannot give them knowledge or competence in general: it is bound to be knowledge *of* something or competence *at* something; it is bound to be some kind, or different kinds, of knowledge and competence. For instance, a child can learn to play football and/or chess and/or badminton, but cannot learn to play them all at the same time, just because they are different games. Similarly, you can teach children about animals and plants or about geology and rock formations, or introduce them to the beauties of the countryside, but you cannot do all these at exactly the same time because they are different kinds of knowledge and experience. You might or might not want to bring them all under one subject title, like perhaps 'nature study' or 'the natural environment', but they would still be different.

This difference is a matter of logic and has nothing to do with wanting to 'break down subject barriers' or any other modern educational idea. It just is the case – it could not be otherwise, whatever you did – that some kinds of interests and questions are different from others. Being interested in why birds migrate is different from being interested in how rocks are formed, and still more different from being interested in what makes a beautiful landscape or what sort of houses would spoil it. Asking about how Hitler rose to power is different from asking about whether Hitler was a good man. Of course, there may be connections between these interests, but they are still different.

These differences are what make 'subjects' inevitable. Suppose you take some children to see a church. Sooner or later, whatever your views about 'subjects', they are going to be interested in it in different ways. Some children will be interested in how it is built or how the spire manages to stay up when it is so tall – that is the start of 'mechanics' or part of 'architecture'. Other children will be interested in who built it and why, how it got to be there, and who wanted it – the start of 'history'. Others may want to know what it is for and what goes on in it – 'religion' or perhaps 'sociology'. And so on. It is inevitable that you should cater for these different interests in different ways simply because they *are* different. If a child asks, 'How does the spire manage to stand up?' and you reply, 'Yes, isn't it beautiful? It cost £5,000 and was built in 1876', you will not be able to educate that child at all; what the child wants to know, now anyway, is something about stresses and structures and building.

So we have to make 'subjects' fit different interests. This is a long and difficult business because many subjects have grown up in a rather haphazard way, not necessarily because of the differences in the particular angles from which people might be interested in things but for quite other reasons. Some of the reasons have to do with our history: for instance, when science became important we began to do less Latin, Greek and theology and more biology, physics and mathematics. Other subjects are studied as a result of tradition or inertia. This gives us a very mixed bag of subject-titles. But what we have to do is not to try to scrap the lot but to look much more closely and carefully at all of them, so that we can find out what we are trying to do. Before we start some major operation that we might call 'changing the curriculum', we have to be clear about what we are doing now, and this brings us inevitably back to questions like 'What is it to teach such and such?'

Now, when we stop to think, we know quite well – or if we do not, Professor Hirst has told us (Hirst and Peters, 1970) – that subject-titles can be of two kinds. First, we can be interested in, and study, some things or phenomena: we may want to know about trees, or motor cars, or what grandfather did when he was a little boy. Subject-titles such as 'the motor car', or 'forestry', or 'race prejudice' are like this. Secondly, we can be interested in looking at lots of things from specific *angles* or by means of specific *disciplines*: for instance, we may be interested in the general business of why things work, in making observations and doing experiments on all sorts of things in the physical world, not anything in particular – in this case, we might call our subject 'science' or 'scientific method'.

It is important to see how different these are. A person's attention might be captured by certain things – say, churches. That person just likes them or is fascinated by them in a general sort of way; likes learning anything to do with them – the history of churches, their architecture, how they are decorated, who goes to them and so on – and might not be interested in other buildings, such as town halls or palaces. Another person is interested less in things than in a particular angle or approach to them; is interested, say, in architecture – not just church architecture but the architecture of all sorts of buildings. This person's attachment is to a particular discipline.

When we ask of any subject 'What is it to teach such and such?' we have to bear this difference very much in mind; otherwise we may be misled by the subject-title. For instance, a pupil who is keen on learning about battles in the Napoleonic Wars might be said to be 'interested in history', and is indeed interested in some of the *phenomena* that we deal with under the title 'history', namely, the battles. We might say the pupil is interested in the history (or some aspects of the history) of the Napoleonic Wars. But is this pupil also interested in 'history' as a discipline, or just interested in battles? To be interested in history as a discipline means to like, in general, to find out things about human activity in the past. Again, to be interested in 'science' ('scientific method') means to be keen on finding out why things happen as they do in the physical world.

So the first thing we have to decide about any subject-title, if we ask 'What is it to teach X?', is whether X is to be the name of a thing or set of phenomena, or the name of a discipline or angle or approach. Sometimes the answer to this is pretty clear. 'Mathematics' or 'logic', for instance, do not name things. Certainly, we could say that mathematics was 'about numbers and figures and so on' or that logic was 'about statements and truth', but more naturally we would say that to learn mathematics was to learn a particular kind of thinking, a set of techniques, a discipline. 'A good mathematician' is somebody who is good at this kind of thinking. Equally obviously, titles like 'the motor car' or 'race prejudice' stand not for particular disciplines but for particular things or phenomena – that is, for motor cars and race prejudice.

But other cases need more thought. 'English' (like 'French' and other titles of the study of languages) seems to refer to certain phenomena; but a title like 'literary criticism' or 'literary appreciation' obviously refers to a kind of discipline, a particular style of thought (which one might use on other literature besides English). 'Science' seems to refer to a discipline, but when we talk of 'biology', 'zoology', 'physics', etc., we indicate that we are using the discipline in a limited way, applying it only to certain things or phenomena and not to others. ('Zoology', for example, is the discipline of science as applied only to living things.) 'History' might be taken to be a discipline, but a course or subject called 'the history of the French Revolution', though it would obviously have to use the discipline of 'history', would refer specifically to a limited range of phenomena – that is, what happened in the French Revolution. Finally, we have to note that quite a few titles – 'classics', 'social studies', 'RE', 'moral education' and plenty of others – are so imprecise that the actual words may not be much of a guide. In some cases it may be more a matter of deciding *what we are going to mean by*, say, 'classics', than of deciding what we *do in fact mean* by it; for there may not be anything very specific which we do mean.

Observe now – this is pretty obvious – that even when the subject-title is the name of a thing (rather than a discipline), you still have to use some discipline in order to study the thing. For instance, 'the motor car' is a 'thing' title, but it is not possible to be interested in motor cars except by being interested in various aspects of them (perhaps in all aspects). At any one time you will be asking questions about one of these different aspects – for instance, about their development over the last 50 years (that is history), or about how they work (that is science), or about their appearance and whether they look nice (that is art appreciation or 'aesthetics'). So – as we saw in the case of pupils who were interested in churches – we cannot avoid having subjects in the sense of 'disciplines', whatever we do with the subject-titles. Thus if we decided to 'get rid of subjects' altogether and wiped all the subject-titles off the notice-board (or replaced them all with a single title like 'life' or 'the world'), we would still have to be clear about what we were doing in any single classroom period, or for the next ten minutes, or for any particular timespan.

So it would obviously be useful to compile a list of the disciplines: that is, a list of the various angles from which pupils can be interested in things, of the kinds of questions and answers and knowledge that apply to different aspects of them. This is not easy because it is not easy to know just how to chop up different kinds of human knowledge and experience. But certainly one of the more promising lists has been made by Hirst (Hirst and Peters, 1970), and it is worth looking at it to see how the disciplines or 'forms of thought' (as he calls them) might relate to subject titles as they appear in school curricula.

1. *Logic/mathematics* This kind of knowledge is not about the world of our sense experience at all but about logical derivations from certain rules or axioms. In some ways, it is like playing a game. You start with the axioms of Euclid or rules about the meaning of certain signs and symbols, and then you derive further knowledge from these. We all have a fairly clear idea what sort of operation this is, and the school subjects that come under the general title 'mathematics' are clear examples of it.

2. *Science* This kind of knowledge is about the physical world, about causes and effects in nature, why things fall downwards, why planets move in ellipses and so on. Again, this is pretty clear, and we can identify this discipline in subjects entitled 'chemistry', or 'physics', or 'biology'.

3. *Personal knowledge* This is more difficult. But you can see that when we ask questions about why *people* do things (not why planets or light waves do things), it is a different sort of study. People have intentions, purposes and plans, which planets do not have. So 'Why did he ...?' means something very different from 'Why did it ...?' And, as we would expect, the sort of evidence with which we need to work is different: for people we need evidence about what goes on in their heads – about their intentions and designs. The clearest case of a subject-title that uses this discipline is 'history', which is surely about why people did things in the past. (If we were interested in why eclipses or earthquakes happened in the past, that would be more like science.) Some aspects of what goes on under title like 'psychology' or 'sociology' may be also concerned with personal knowledge, though other aspects may be more like science: it all depends what sort of answers and knowledge we are after.

4. *Morality, aesthetics and religion* These are more difficult still. We lump them together partly because it is not clear what ground each of

the three words covers, and there may be some overlap. (Thus for some people 'morality' is part of 'religion', or at least importantly connected with it.) But it seems plausible to say that there are questions about what is morally right and wrong, which are different from questions about what is beautiful, or ugly, or dainty, or elegant ('aesthetics'), and perhaps different again from questions about what one should worship or pray to ('religion'). Philosophers have been working on these areas, trying to help us get clearer about them, but even now we can see that some subject-titles include some of the disciplines. Thus if under the title of 'English' I try to get children to appreciate the elegance or effectiveness of a poem or a play, that looks like 'aesthetics' – and it is similar to (the same sort of discipline as) what the French teacher might do with a French poem or what the music teacher might do in musical appreciation classes.

It is worth noting here, incidentally, that not being as clear as we ought to be about these disciplines holds up all possible progress in some cases. The most obvious example is RE. We have the subject title 'RE' (or 'RI' or 'scripture' or 'divinity' or anything we like to choose), but it does not help unless we know what *sort* of knowledge – what discipline – is involved in teaching RE. We can sidestep the problem by, say, teaching church history in RE periods, but that is the discipline of history or personal knowledge and might well be left to the history teachers; or we can encourage children to appreciate the beauty of biblical language, but that is the discipline of aesthetics or literary appreciation and might well be left to the English teacher. Religious people at least will feel that there is something missing if that is all we do. The problem for such people is to point out a special kind of discipline, with a special kind of knowledge, that should go on under 'RE'.

This kind of list is very useful to bear in mind when we are considering rather vaguely entitled new subjects, as perhaps 'social studies' or 'the environment' or 'sex education'. For we at once want to know what disciplines are going to be involved, and the list allows us to raise the question against a useful background. Is 'sex education', for instance, going to be just science (teaching about biology and contraception and so on)? Or are we going to bring in personal knowledge also (helping pupils to understand their own and other people's feelings)? And are we going to raise questions about what is right and wrong (morality)? These can all be seen as different issues. Until we are clear about which disciplines we are going to bring in, these subject titles will be hopelessly vague.

It is remarkable how many subject-titles there are in school curricula that do not fit neatly into any single discipline. Mathematics, the sciences and perhaps history fit clearly enough into identifiable categories, but consider again titles like 'English', 'classics', 'geography', 'French' and so on. It seems pretty clear that these subjects involve a number of different disciplines. Sometimes it is also clear what the disciplines are: 'geography', for instance, is 'science' in so far as we ask questions about the physical world ('physical geography') and 'personal knowledge' when we ask about why people do things ('human geography'). But often even this is not very clear. Try working out what disciplines might be involved in 'English', 'French', 'classics' or, indeed, in learning to read and write. It is not so easy.

Fortunately, there are other ways in which we can get clearer about 'what it is to teach such-and-such'. One way is to take a closer look at the particular body of knowledge or set of abilities that is normally associated with the subject-title. It is important to realize here that though some subject-titles are more vague than others, normally not just anything counts as 'teaching such-and-such'. (You might get away with almost anything under an extremely vague title like 'the environment' but not with more usual titles like 'English' or 'French'.) Thus we would not normally talk of someone being good at English or knowing a lot about English if he could not spell simple English words, or could not write clear English sentences or had not heard of Shakespeare or Dickens; these seem pretty central to the idea of 'English', and we can say this even though we may not be completely clear about exactly what disciplines, from Hirst's list or from any other logical list of the kind, are involved.

We are suggesting, then, that the best starting-point for teachers who want to be clear about what it is to teach a particular subject is to take the subject-title seriously. If you start in this way, it gradually becomes clear which different kinds of knowledge and abilities are involved – what the differences between them are – and then we can give them more appropriate titles, if these do not already exist. In doing this, you have to compare what the subject-title suggests with what does (or might) actually go on in school periods; often this has alarming results, as in the case of RE. (If in an RE period a teacher discussed the problems of homeless people, or sex, or the history of the Bible, we should want to ask, 'But can we fairly describe that as education in *religion*?' The title 'RE' does not match up to what is actually discussed in the period.)

Teachers of various subjects must do this job of sorting out titles and practices for themselves (it would take far too long here), but we will take one example to make the task clearer. Suppose we have 'French' on the timetable. We look round at what happens in schools and find that different people do different things: (a) get the pupils to speak and understand ordinary French orally (perhaps in a language laboratory or by sending them to French families); (b) get them to read and write French correctly; (c) acquaint them with the classics of French literature (Racine and Molière and so on); (d) explain to them how modern French grew out of Latin, via medieval French; (e) familiarize them with the French way of life and the countryside of France; (f) explain to them various aspects of French history, politics and geography; (g) try to make them less prejudiced about the French people and more in favour of the European Union;

(h) take them for a canoe trip down the Rhône; (i) give them a good time in Paris for a weekend.

We need to start by asking, 'Which of these count as "learning French"?' We would accept (a) and (b) without much hesitation and perhaps classify them more clearly under 'the French language'. If we wanted to bring in (c), we should have to make this clear by saying 'French literature' (you can 'know French' without knowing anything about French literature). With (d) we might hesitate a bit: it is not 'learning French' exactly, but it gives pupils a better and fuller understanding of why modern French is as it is: perhaps we can classify it under 'the French language'. With (e) and (f) we should hesitate a good deal more: these things might sometimes be relevant to 'learning French' (for instance, you might have to see the Normandy countryside to understand properly what *bocage* means) but perhaps not very often. They are more like (g), which is really concerned not with 'learning French' at all but rather with moral education or the education of the emotions, or perhaps politics or economics. Items (h) and (i), again, are not part of what is meant by 'learning French' – they may (or may not) be good ways of getting pupils interested in 'learning French', but that is different. (And this is a very important difference: teachers may have to do all sorts of things to get their pupils interested in a subject, but that is not the same as actually teaching it.)

In this example we have roughly sorted out nine activities, (a) to (i), that are candidates for part of what is meant, or might be meant, by 'learning French'. We have left out all sorts of other candidates, and we have separated them or sorted them far too casually and roughly; but it is very important that we start in this way because what we need first (in the case of any subject-title) is a clear list of different things that are not aims of 'teaching French' but part of what it is to teach French or what might be thought to be part of it. It is only too easy to avoid this task and to try to produce lists of objectives in a high-minded and muddled way. This leads to chaos. For instance, we might compile a list of objectives that included these items: to assist the pupils' understanding of French culture and literature; to familiarize the pupils with French thought and life; to give them a sound working knowledge of the language and thereby to improve their self-expression and ability to communicate with others; to acquaint them with the best and most profound writings in French, both past and present; and so on. You can see how useless this exercise is. First, half the time this list has its eye on 'external' aims (e.g. 'to improve their self-expression') and not on what it is to teach French. But worse, the items on the list overlap hopelessly. If we 'familiarize the pupils with French thought', do we not thereby 'assist the pupils' understanding of French culture and literature'? And is not that also partly the same as acquainting them 'with the best and most profound writings in French'? Unless the items on such lists are discrete – that is, logically distinct and separate from each other – the lists are useless.

Of course, items (a) to (i) on our list are only a start, but at least they are different, and at least we can start to form some fairly clear concepts of what falls within the notion 'teaching French' and what does not. Thus we allow, let us suppose, (a), (b), (c) and (d), but not the rest. We could in principle run the same sort of operation for 'teaching English', 'mathematics' and anything else – though in some cases, like perhaps 'classics', the title would be so vague that we might be in more doubt. (Yet even here we have some idea of what counts: if a teacher spent all his or her time telling pupils about classic race meetings or films shown as the Classic Cinema, we should say either that the teacher was a rogue or that he or she did not know what 'classics' meant in education).

Now this is a start, but of course it does not solve all our curricular problems (though it may in itself help teachers to be clear about their own subjects at least). For now we think,

> Very well, we have a clearer idea of what's meant by 'teaching X'. But do the things that fall *outside* that concept – (e), (f), (g) and so on – have to be written off? Might not they be very important? Ought not they to be catered for somehow?

This thought is quite right. But the point is that as a result of making such a list and seeing the differences and distinctions between the very various things that we can do with pupils, we begin to see more clearly what sort of thing each is, and perhaps how in principle we might cater for it (not necessarily in French lessons).

Take (e), for instance – the item about familiarizing pupils with the French countryside. This may be important, but would it not be better done under the heading of 'geography'? Or (g), trying to diminish their prejudice: why on earth should we try to do this under the heading of 'learning French'? Why not get down to the job of trying to determine what produces or diminishes racial prejudice and have special periods about it – or perhaps not periods at all but some other approach altogether (role-playing, or visits to French families)? Or (i), the Paris weekend: if our idea is to give pupils a good time – and why not, every now and then? – that is fair enough, but there might be a cheaper and better way.

If we look at these differences and distinctions hard enough, we shall begin to make sense of how to cater for our aims, and this is of practical value in two ways. First, we cater for our aims more effectively by understanding them and giving them importance in their own right: and second, we avoid messing up existing subjects by bringing in irrelevant and extraneous issues. For instance, suppose we are looking at 'English' or 'English literature'. One of the things that might emerge, if we make a list, could be something like 'getting the pupils to understand and sympathize with other people': a very worthy aim, but not obviously central to the notion of 'teaching English'. This fits better under some title like 'moral education'. If we do not fit it in there, where it belongs, two bad things happen. First, we do not cater properly for moral education but just vaguely hope it happens in 'English' periods; and, second, we do not concentrate properly on 'teaching English' because we vaguely feel we have to do moral education as well in those periods. This is a muddle and does nobody any good.

The task is obviously a vast and complex one and not necessarily to be undertaken by particular subject teachers (though they can help with it). Let us assume that, some of the time, we are getting on with the task – that is, trying to get clear about, and cater for things that *do not* count as 'teaching X' itself: then there are still some other considerations to be remembered, not yet mentioned. We still do not mean consideration of 'method' (or of 'aims'): we mean considerations about what it is to teach (or learn) X. There are two ways in particular.

First, it is not always as easy as we have made it sound to say what counts as X and what does not. We have to keep X separated from other subjects or disciplines – as when we say, 'But surely that's really geography', or 'That's not really English; it's moral education'. But we also have to keep X separated from very general sorts of knowledge, or abilities, or character traits. For instance, if a pupil has a speech impediment and finds difficulty in talking, the French (or English) teacher might try to cope with this by teaching the child to speak French (or English). Certainly, being able to speak French involves being able to speak in general, but this general ability is not part of learning French as such.

To take a more difficult example, suppose we have a title like 'mathematics'. Now, when we teach children about fractions or multiplication or decimals we have no doubt that these are 'mathematics'. But suppose we have a child who does not see that if A is bigger than B and B is bigger than C, then A is bigger than C, or a child who seems to think that somehow there is 'more' water when you pour it from a short fat vessel into a tall thin one, as in Piaget's experiments. We are dealing here with very general notions about space and volume and logic – do these really come under 'mathematics'? This would be like saying that teaching a child what 'yesterday' means comes under 'history'.

There are lots of questions of this kind (and no single, simple answers to them). All we are doing here is to point to the difficulty of determining the cut-off point (so to speak) at which we are going to say, 'That's not teaching such-and-such specifically; that's trying to give the child more intelligence, or certain very general concepts which he needs for any subject, or the ability to concentrate in general'. There must be such cut-off points, otherwise we can fix no clear idea at all of any subject as such. A subject teacher needs a clear idea of what being able to learn his subject *presupposes*, if only in order to distinguish that from what learning his subject consists of. This has to be worked out in each case.

Second, a different kind of consideration, but one that is of immense importance for practical teaching: even assuming that we are quite clear about the boundary lines of a subject, we can still emphasize certain aspects at the expense of others. We do not mean by 'aspects' different parts of the subject – for instance, spelling as against oral communication in English, or algebra rather than geometry in mathematics. We are referring, rather, to the different kinds of interest a pupil or teacher might have in a subject or (better) the different ways in which they might see the subject.

This is not easy to explain, though we all have a fairly clear idea of it in a way. For example, one mathematics teacher may be comparatively uninterested in whether pupils really understand the basic logic and concepts behind various operations, such as multiplying fractions and solving equations, and is worried only about whether they can actually conduct the operations – whether they can multiply fractions and solve equations. Such a teacher might say 'Never mind why x squared minus y squared can be written $(x - y) (x + y)$, just do it'. Another teacher may not mind so much about what the pupils can do – whether they can do long division and remember formulae for working out areas – as long as they really have a grasp of the concepts involved.

Again, one Latin teacher may just present his class with the words *Arma virumque cano* and say, 'That means "I sing of arms and the man"', without worrying about the grammar and construction. Another might say, '*Arma* is in the accusative, object of *cano*: *vir* means "a man" as opposed to a woman, here perhaps something more like "a hero"', and so on. The first wants to get on with it so to speak – s/he is interested in getting the pupils to grasp the general flow of meaning – whereas the second wants to make sure that they really know how the language works. (We might say the first is more interested in getting across what Virgil is saying, the second is more interested in Latin. Or a French teacher might say, 'Never mind about the grammar of what you're saying. Just make the noises of *Merci mille fois, monsieur*'. Or a history teacher might say,

> The Normans invaded in 1066 and their duke became the first English king ... No, never mind for the moment who the Normans were, children, or why they were called Normans, or exactly what a duke is (he's a sort of leader). Let's get on with what happened.

Other French and history teachers might prefer to stop and work out things in more detail before going on.

We want to make it clear, again, that we are not talking about the best method of teaching children the same content, but really about different contents. Thus I might learn everything about chess either by having all the moves and pieces explained to me first and then playing, or by starting to play much sooner and picking up the moves and other details as I play. Which method suits me best is a matter of technique (and/or my own temperament). But with subjects it can be different. One person, for instance, may be very good at doing things in mathematics (mental arithmetic, solving equations, etc.) but without much grasp of the logic of the operations; another may understand all about set theory and the basic axioms of mathematics but be hopeless at performing with them because this person has not been given the teaching or the practice. One person may be able to give a reasonable account of what Virgil's *Aeneid* is about but be quite unable to construe one line of it; another may be good at working out just how the words fit but not know much about the poem as a whole.

Again, there is no single 'answer' to this – that is, no question of its always being right to 'get on with it' or always being right to understand everything first. This would lead to absurdity. To understand *everything* about the words *Arma virumque cano*, we should have to go into why these words had the form they did in classical Latin, all the various meanings of *vir* (with parallels from other authors), the basic roots and derivations of the words and so on, just as to understand everything in even the simplest mathematics operation would, strictly speaking, take us right back to the logical foundations or philosophy of mathematics. On the other hand, without some understanding we should have nothing but parroted learning – the pupils would not really acquire any knowledge at all, except knowledge of how to make appropriate noises.

This sort of dimension runs through all subjects: it is difficult, and may be misleading, to describe the opposite ends of it all, but we might briefly call one end 'wanting to get to the root of it' and the other end 'wanting to get on with it'. It is likely that nearly all children have both desires in them, and certainly all subjects include both these aspects. For the practising teacher it is a matter of how far he wants to go along this dimension in either direction. One way is not necessarily better than the other, but it can be very different. Thus there is a lot of difference between someone who can speak good French but has never thought, or been taught, about why some words are right in some places and others wrong, and someone who can give a good account of French grammar and syntax but is bad at speaking; or between the person who knows about Latin culture and poetry but does not know much Latin and the person who can read and write Latin fluently but knows nothing about Virgil, Horace or Cicero. These differences can be (as here) so big that they virtually break the subject down into two separate topics.

All we can do here – and it is important to do it – is to get these differences sorted out as clearly as possible in each subject. Only then can we make guesses about what is likely to interest the children, what it might be important for them to know and – once we have settled that – how we can best teach it. Here, as elsewhere, it is essential to do the thinking first and not rush ahead too quickly with discussing 'methods'. For, as you may see by now, we are not always clear about what our subjects are in the first place or about what it is to teach this or that subject.

Chapter 7

Making subjects interesting

Teachers and student teachers are commonly enjoined to make what they teach interesting to their pupils (indeed much of their training is devoted to helping them to achieve this aim); and, just as commonly (indeed, almost universally), the sense of this injunction is regarded as non-controversial. On reflection, however, as I shall try to show, it seems not only controversial but deeply paradoxical. A proper resolution of the paradox is of central importance to all learning.

I

The paradox is this: suppose we agree on something which we want the pupils to learn (it makes no difference whether we talk here of 'subjects', 'skills', 'content', 'knowing that', 'knowing how', or anything else). Then either (a) we dress it up in borrowed clothes to give it a more attractive external appearance: but then what we are presenting to the pupils is not the subject itself but some (false) image of the subject; or else (b) we change the inner constitution of the subject into something which is more likely to catch the interest of our pupils, in which case we are not making the original subject interesting (or anything else) at all. For instance, if we want the pupils to learn Latin and Greek, either (a) we try to attract their interest by putting up glossy pictures of the Parthenon or wounded Gauls, in which case we are not making the Latin and Greek languages interesting, or (b) we change the substance behind titles like 'classics' or 'Latin', forgetting about the (we think, boring) complexities of Latin grammar and substituting the (we hope, more interesting) topics of slavery in the ancient world or Roman aqueducts. In neither case, it seems, have we made *Latin* interesting.

That this is not peculiar to subjects (in the educational sense of the word) can be seen if we consider the case of making oneself more interesting as a person. In the extensive popular literature on this topic, two sorts of recommendations are offered to me if I want to succeed socially, or become more popular, or perhaps more attractive sexually. I can either (a) dress myself up (literally and metaphorically) and 'improve my image', but then I am no longer making my real self more interesting, and run the risk of losing authenticity, integrity or even honesty (something which puritanical or iconoclastic traditions have taken very seriously in past history); or (b) I can change myself, perhaps becoming more extroverted and sociable, altering my personality or even my character; but then it is no longer my original self that I am making more interesting – and that alternative may seem even more inauthentic and corrupting than the other. *Prima facie* there seems to be no way out of this.

II

The paradox is dissolved only when we make some sort of distinction between features of a person, or of a subject to be learned, that we are going to count as 'dressing up' (the thing's image) on the one hand, and features which can reasonably be seen as part of the thing itself. To take another example, suppose we say that we want to make church services more interesting. Then we might (a) 'dress up' the church externally, advertising it with lurid neon signs or beckoning blondes – but these (we presume) give a false image of the service itself; or, worse, (b) change the church service into something which appeals to the baser desires of the congregation – but then we have an orgy and not the worship of God. But there is also option (c); *presenting* or *arranging* the worship in a certain way which is more interesting than it might be, and which so far from producing false images actually *expresses* the intentions of the service more fully. Good religious music, church architecture, ritual, and liturgical features in general do not distract from worship but, as it were, give it a proper shape; just as the right kind of clothes, perhaps even cosmetics, need not falsify the nature of the person who wears them, nor even be a merely temporary adjunct, but can reasonably be seen as part of the person.

The idea of arrangement enables us to escape our paradox, because there is here no question either of dressing up a subject or of altering its essential features or inner constitution. In its simplest form, making a subject interesting could consist just of arranging those features in the most appealing or attractive way; we can reshuffle the cards without changing the pack as a whole. Here, of course, at least with most (I think all) subjects, we are constrained by certain necessary logical sequences in learning: certain concepts and practices have to be learned before others. Nevertheless, there is a good deal of latitude. It is arguable, for instance, whether it is better to start at the beginning of a historical period and work forwards, thus developing the narrative in a natural way, or to start at the end and work backwards, thus encouraging the search for causes; or whether it is better to start the learning of Latin with the basic grammar and work towards translation of a text, or to start with a (simple) text and work back to the grammatical features. These are questions of pedagogic strategy or tactics; but they are real questions, even if we do not often know the answers.

III

Nevertheless, there are fairly severe limits on what can be achieved by arrangement; and there is also the danger that, in trying to rearrange subjects so as to attract pupils' interest, we may fall foul of the two dangers already mentioned – either we dress up the subject with false images, or we alter its necessary constitution. More progress is likely to be made if we reflect on the point, obvious in itself but rarely pursued in depth and detail, that if a person is interested in something for its own sake there must be some kind of psychological (and perhaps logical, see below) marriage between what constitutes that thing and certain features of his unconscious mind. Here the idea of making subjects *interesting* is itself likely to be corrupting: the term suggests a slightly superficial and temporary attachment as against a long-term commitment. Anyone who was really wedded to a subject, really on the inside of it, would not, of course, deny that they found it interesting, but would hardly speak of their relation to it in those terms. There is something odd in saying that Wittgenstein was *interested* in philosophy, or Einstein in physics, or Mozart in music.

Two lines of enquiry suggest themselves here, both stemming from the somewhat stronger notion of being in love with, or truly loving, a subject for its own sake. The first would involve a serious investigation of the possible marriages, mentioned above, between the subject and the unconscious: we need to know what there is *in* or *about* Latin, geography, mathematics, etc. that can be displayed as permanently thrilling, glamorous, romantic, engrossing or compelling. Here we turn naturally, and rightly, to clinical psychology or psychiatry, and ask questions like 'From what childhood desires flows the kind of excitement and commitment some people have to (say) making and reading maps, or playing with shapes and numbers, or working out verbal puzzles?' General accounts of motivation, which employ overall ideas like 'curiosity' or 'achievement motivation', are of little help here, because they are neither deep enough nor specific enough to explain the very particular and profound marriages that do (if too rarely) occur. Certain people are virtually driven or compelled by certain subjects or forms or fields of knowledge, and we need to know why. We also need to know more about the conditions under which the marriages occur, not only about their constituents: sometimes there is a sort of *coup de foudre*, in which a person suddenly falls in love with something; sometimes a vital spark is struck after a longer acquaintance. (The parallel with falling in love with a person is not, I think, just a parallel: the same constituents and conditions are likely to apply in both cases.)

But no advances in this kind of psychological enquiry can be fruitful unless we are clearer about one partner in such marriages: namely, what there is in the subjects themselves. Very little has been written on this topic, chiefly because it is immensely difficult to *say* just why one loves Latin or geography or whatever. (Though, I must add, it is partly also because the idea of subjects being important and glamorous in themselves is not a fashionable one; more usually the desire to integrate subjects and teach 'skills' rather than 'content' – as if the two were separable – inhibits even the attempt.) The enthusiasm for a subject, which teachers are rightly enjoined to display, needs to be given a *shape* which directs pupils' attention to its inherently glamorous or love-compelling features, and it is important to be as consciously clear as possible about just what these are. To some extent this is a philosophical or phenomenological task, not a psychological or empirical one. We need to ask, as I said above, just what there is about *Latin* (as against not only Ancient Greek but a modern language) which could compel commitment: and, in fact, there are things one could say about this (the peculiar economy of Latin, its particular sonority, lapidary quality, elegance and so forth). Clearer ideas about these peculiarities can, of course, emerge effectively not so much in direct articulation to pupils about them, but in showing them, contrasting them and in general making them more visible in practical pedagogy.

A thorough study of individual subjects from this viewpoint would get us a long way. Amongst other things, it might enable us to answer questions about the suitability of particular subjects for particular pupils. We are at present totally uncertain whether, in the case of certain types of pupils, the truth is that (because of their emotional constitution) they will never fall in love with this or that subject, or rather that they are capable of doing so if the subject is properly displayed to them. One might incline to believe that, at least in principle, the riches and excitement which (plainly) exist in all subjects (because some people at least fall genuinely in love with them) can be made available to all people: that all blind spots can be cleared up if only we knew how to make the excitement more easily visible. But, of course, that may be a romantic view; perhaps, just as some people are tone-deaf, some people are constitutionally incapable of being moved by science, or poetry, or whatever.

The second line of enquiry also challenges the potential corruption of the term 'interesting', but from a different angle. Permanent attachments may be engendered by deeply glamorous features of what one is attached to, but are not solely sustained by those features, which in any case are not effectively operative all the time. In the (frequent) gaps, it is not so much the ideas represented by 'duty' or 'commitment' that sustain the attachment, but the ideas of 'belonging' or 'identification'. The person sees the object of attachment as his or her own, as part of him or her (for richer or for poorer, in sickness and in health). Just as one may see one's home, or country, or blood relations as somehow constituting one's identity, so one may see oneself as in some way bound up with the pursuit of literature, or philosophy, or mathematics or whatever. One sees them as part of one's life, not (or not only) as things one is interested in some of the time and bored with on other occasions.

We need to think here of subjects as forms of *life*, not just a form of knowledge and certainly not just as some mixture of 'skills' and 'content'. Children fortunately brought up in families which spend a lot of time reading and writing and playing word-games, or singing and listening to music and playing instruments, see these activities as normal features of everyday life. There is indeed something artificial, perhaps corrupting, in trying to reduce or organize these into 40-minute classroom periods labelled 'literature' or 'musical appreciation': if we ask how *those* (40-minute) forms of life can be seen as glamorous, or become permanent parts of a pupil's identity, we are likely to get only dusty answers. We ought rather to ask questions like 'What would a school (or any community) look like if it devoted itself entirely for (say) a month to immersing its members in literature/science/music/French, etc.?' or 'How can pupils be given permanent and habitual responsibility for pursuing literature/science etc., in their daily lives in and out of school?' It is surely clear that the answers to these questions may not lie solely, or even primarily, along the lines of putting pupils through a set of classroom periods for five or six hours every day.

IV

There are two notions that lie under our suggestions so far: the notions traditionally represented by *eros* on the one hand and *philia* on the other. Both of these are fairly high-temperature notions, and contrast with the weaker ideas of a pupil finding a subject 'interesting' or of a subject being 'suitable' for him or her. These weaker ideas remind one of what may be achieved by computer dating or arranged marriages in the field of personal relationships: roughly, a mutual co-extensiveness of interests and suitability, a sound basis for 'getting on with each other' by a proper match of individual characteristics. This is not at all to be sneezed at; and if one regarded marriage (as perhaps one should) as primarily a device for bringing up children in an atmosphere of mutual compatibility and benevolent coexistence, we might want to search no further. As with a choice of marriage partners, or a choice of careers, so with the choice of subjects: we may feel that we are asking too much if we ask for the pupil both to be romantically in love (*eros*) with a subject and to weave it thoroughly into his or her life (*philia*). Not everyone puts a large part of their emotional money on curricular subjects, any more than that on their job or marriage partner. Should we hope for no more than the pupils will be interested, moderately involved, able and willing to rub along with some subjects, pass examinations in them, and so forth, just as they rub along in their jobs and marriages?

One difficulty with this is that there are lifelong incentives for sustaining jobs and marriages – anyone who wants to earn a living and to enjoy family life will be, as it were, kept up to the mark as they rub along: they cannot easily just drop the whole thing. But with curricular subjects the case is different. There may be extrinsic pressures here, such as the need for qualifications or the desire to succeed academically; but these pressures fall away, for the most part, fairly early in life – and then, if there is no intrinsic attachment, no *eros* or *philia*, the subjects are in fact simply dropped, as they are by the vast majority of pupils. Educators then find themselves reduced to offering incentives which may be even more despicable than the (at least realistic) need for qualifications: pupils may be told that it is more 'cultured', or respectable, to read books rather than play bingo, or to prefer burgundy to beer. Like some marriages, the attachment will be for the sake of social form, with nothing genuine between two individuals at all.

But in any case, the joys of genuine attachment are such that we would naturally search very hard before abandoning the quest. Many progressive educators have, quite rightly, lamented the enormous wastage and fruit-lessness in school learning: it has seemed to them, again rightly, that many of all subjects taught are *dead* for the children, and this has presented itself primarily under descriptions like 'boring', 'unappealing' or 'uninteresting'. However, such educators (as I hinted above) have commonly ascribed this to the vast amount of 'dead' content in the subjects, so that they have been wrongly led to make two moves: (1) to diminish 'content' in favour of 'skills', and (2) to diminish the uniqueness of subjects in favour of some sort of merging or 'integration'. But this tackles the problem the wrong way round. The commonly expressed idea that subjects are not 'relevant' to the pupils, though excessively vague, is not vacuous: it is a way of saying that the subjects are not (as we put it) woven into their lives. But there are two ways of dealing with this. We can either (a) change the *subjects*, along the (I think mistaken) lines just mentioned; or (b) change the pupils' *lives*, at least to the extent of weaving the subjects into them.

I have been arguing for (b), which takes us in a radically different direction from what usually comes to mind when we talk of 'making subjects interesting'. The difference emerges clearly, for instance, if we consider the learning of a (non-natural) language. Few would deny that a comparatively short time spent in (say) a French family achieves much better results, even of a superficial kind, than many hours of classroom study in which French is 'made interesting'; and this is quite evidently because the pupil is immersed in a form of life which at least gives him or her the chance to take the language fully into his or her mind and heart. The learning of a natural language offers an even stronger example. As many authors (see particularly Hamlyn, 1978) have stressed, the process is indissolubly linked with a certain form of life in which the child's closest speakers (the parents) not only speak to the child but act with and for him or her. The child does not find the language 'interesting', and little or nothing is gained by the parents' trying to make it so. Rather, there is love (and hence, plenty of rewarding interaction) between them; the child both imitates and is initiated into the language so that it forms a permanent part of his or her personality. Here it may seem in a way superficial even to talk of *eros* or *philia*; the imitation and initiation actually create the child's self, rather than flow from a self which is already created and desires an additional marriage.

Amongst crucial elements here is, obviously enough, the psychological closeness of the child with his or her parents: something which we have somehow to reproduce in schools if we are to succeed at all. There is also the feature that the child is initiated into – indeed, lives with – a *community* whose normal life includes and partly consists of the form of life in question (the use of language, or scientific enquiry, or moral discussion, or whatever). These features, strikingly absent from many schools, are far removed from another idea which has misled progressive educationalists – the idea that pupils' engagement, their opportunity for *eros* and *philia* in forms of life, is enhanced by freedom of choice. Growing children are in no serious sense *free* to learn or not to learn a natural language: they learn because of the necessity – one hopes, a necessity which they welcome, but still a necessity – to participate in the life of their parents and older siblings. So too, in a slightly diminished form, if a child has to exist in a French family for a longish period of time when older: opting out of the family's life altogether is hardly a real possibility. So, again, if the child is (with or without his or her consent) immersed in classical music in a household where such music is constantly played. If, as progressive educators rightly note, there is a disconnection between the pupil's life and the subjects he or she is supposed to learn, then of course we may argue either (1) that the child should be free to give or withhold his or her consent to learning, or (2) that the child should be, despite the disconnection, forced to learn. But each of these is a *pis aller*: we have to remove the original disconnection.

Even the idea of 'motivation', like the idea of 'interest', can be out of place here, because it suggests an option which will only be taken up if some special 'motivational' factor is present. A great deal of what we do – and this applies to learning as well as other activities – is not 'motivated' in this sense at all; it is, rather, a matter of habit or participation. We should think here, not so much of increasing pupils' freedom of choice, but of a fairly well-structured environment in which such habits are formed largely by their being taken for granted. Our model for schools here should be something much more like an active and well-ordered family which operates warmly but demandingly as a group, and much less like a well-stocked supermarket where the consumer can buy whatever takes his or her fancy.

V

Much of what I have said above can be seen just as an extension – I hope, a useful one – of what other philosophers have more eloquently expressed. It is not clear, however, that it has or has had much practical effect on schools. This is partly because the central points are not widely enough appreciated, but partly also because we are not clear enough in identifying the opposition. A good deal of further work is needed in clarifying the pressures which make us overlook the points, or fail to put them into practice. Other disciplines besides philosophy – those concerned with the politics, economics and psychopathology of educational institutions – are needed here; but a philosopher may perhaps help with an initial taxonomy. There are, for instance, two obvious categories which seem to have some items as obvious candidates for inclusion, as follows:

1. *External* enemies and social forms militate strongly against the central educational practice of a close-knit learning community (along Socratic or family lines). The pressures of bureaucracy, excessive time spent on evaluation and assessment, committee meetings, and the timetabling of school periods all play a part here, leaving little time for such (perhaps fairly simple) structures as are needed if pupils are to be thoroughly engaged in the way described earlier. These pressures have simply to be resisted, particularly at a time when many teachers are frightened and demoralized, and have lost confidence in the central practice. A clear and pragmatic sociological account of how this can best be done would be immensely valuable.
2. *Internal* pressures, mostly in the form of educational fantasies, are just as powerful. Amongst these are some already mentioned – an excessive attachment to freedom of choice for pupils, to 'dressing up' subjects or altering their constitution in an endeavour to 'make them interesting', to denying (consciously or unconsciously) the particular and *sui generis* nature and traditions of particular subjects in favour of 'integration', the (falsely antithesized) emphasis on 'skills' as against 'content', and others from the same stable. These pressures have to be psychiatrically understood, faced and overcome; and here again a more detailed and well-tabulated account is badly needed.

For those who – in teacher education, educational administration or elsewhere – are concerned to overcome the opposition and drive home the central points, there are also many methodological or pedagogic questions to answer. How, for instance, does one best convey understanding of a genuine engagement or marriage in education to those (alas, very many) students who have never had the experience of it? Must institutions of teacher training themselves be learning communities of the kind described – something which would call for very radical changes? What kind of attachments to tutors in such institutions do students need to have? How should the students be grouped, and what disciplines (philosophy? psychology? sociology?) are most relevant to their gaining such understanding? Philosophers have a part to play in answering such questions, if only to ensure that they are in fact asked: but teamwork is clearly needed if the answers are to be anything like adequate. I have tried here only to outline the main points from which such a team needs to start work.

Part III

The school community

Chapter 8

Discipline and authority

I WHAT DISCIPLINE IS

All teachers and educators have to face and put into practice certain necessary concepts and principles which are connected with the nature of education itself. Such principles are located in an area marked by such terms as 'discipline', 'control', 'keeping order', etc., and it is no accident that this is also an area in which some of the most serious day-to-day worries of practising teachers crop up. Here we shall have a look at one concept, which I take to be normally marked by 'discipline' and which has (so far as I can see) been almost entirely overlooked by contemporary writers, even though a great deal has been said under this title.

Consider first the notion of a group of people or an institution being well *organized* for a particular purpose. One can have a well-organized classroom, or army, or operating theatre, or youth camp: this has to do with the *arrangements*, perhaps even more specifically with what one might call the *administrative* arrangements, which facilitate the purpose. A youth camp is badly organized if the latrines are too far away (or too near): an operating theatre, if it is not arranged that the assistant with the scalpel stands near enough to the surgeon: a classroom, if the desks do not give the children a clear view of the board. To describe all this under the heading 'discipline' is palpably absurd. Now consider the notion of being trouble-free, or in a broad sense 'controlled'. We get trouble-free prisoners by putting them in chains; trouble-free children by slipping them tranquillizers; trouble-free surgical assistants, perhaps by paying them enough for them not to worry about their mortgage during the operation. Again, this has nothing specifically to do with discipline. And we could run similar arguments with other notions applicable to groups of people: 'having high morale', 'enthusiastic', 'interested', and so on.

'Accepting rules' is much nearer the target, because it brings in the notion of *obedience*. When we talk about the discipline of, say, an army being good, we are not talking about whether its administrative arrange-ments are good, or whether the soldiers are trouble-free and quiescent, or whether their morale and enthusiasm are high – though all these may, contingently, affect discipline or reflect it. We are talking about whether they obey the rules. Perhaps something more than that, however: whether they can be *relied on* to obey the rules. Suppose we have soldiers who do obey the rules, only they do so rather slothfully and mutter curses under their breath and so on. Well, that is better than not obeying them, and certainly they are more well *disciplined* than soldiers who conduct wildly enthusiastic charges against the enemy on their own initiative. But we might think that their discipline was a bit suspect, or 'about to crack', or 'slack', or something like that. We are not just concerned with their overt obedience, but with some kind of disposition to obey.

We are already far away from the idea of maintenance of general conditions of order without which some activity (teaching, fighting) cannot go on, and far away also from any idea that all the rules we want them to obey are of the general form 'don't cause trouble'. A soldier *qua* soldier has of course to obey some rules which have this sort of point (not getting drunk, malingering, etc.); but this soldier also has duties of a different kind – to become proficient with weapons, be able to read a map, etc. Fighting can go on all right without these; but he or she would not be a well-disciplined soldier who did not obey whatever rules enjoined these duties on him or her: just as a pupil would not be a well-disciplined pupil if he or she did not make a sufficient effort, at least, to do the work he or she was ordered to do.

Whatever we may want to do about the *words*, there is clearly a particular concept at stake here: roughly, the notion of *obedience* to *established and legitimate authorities as such*. One could say a very great deal about the practical importance of grasping this notion and making it part of one's life and behaviour; indeed, it is difficult to see how, without this, any institution or society can do more than rely upon the *ad hoc* variety of bribes or threats that might get things done – Mr X's appearance, Miss Y's charm, payment for doing good homework, electric shocks, or whatever else we may wish to deploy. But quite apart from any question of the inefficiency or fragility of such pressures, to omit the notion of dis-cipline in this sense is to omit a whole swathe of concepts (authority, punishment, contract, law and so on) which are logically inevitable for rational creatures.

To accept rules as authoritative, in the sense required for discipline, consists partly in accepting them as *reasons for action*; and this is verified by whether, in the practical situations involved, the motivating thought is something like 'It's a rule' rather than anything else – for example 'It's a good idea', 'I shall suffer if I don't obey', 'I like doing this sort of thing', etc. Whether this is in fact what I have called the 'motivating thought' can, at least in principle, be established by setting up enough controlled situations in which the irrelevant variables do not apply: we see how the subject thinks and acts when it is a bad rule, when the subject will not suffer for disobedience, and so on.

Discipline is concerned with the consistency and strength of these on-the-spot acceptances or cases of obedience to authority. This of course involves or presumes his or her overall acceptance of the authority as such: but it does not involve any question about *why* the subject accepts it. There may be all kinds of reasons why a person accepts or submits to a source of power. I may do this in something like total freedom, as perhaps when I decide to learn French and put myself in the hands of a French teacher. Or, more commonly, I may think that the existing political authorities, rotten though they are, represent the only practically desirable alternative at the present time, and so consent to their rules. Or I may simply find myself (perhaps more commonly still) in a situation where I have no immediate means of escape from the authorities or powers that be, and opt to 'play their game' either because it is the best I can do for myself or because of mere inertia. Many other possibilities exist. The analogy with games, weak at some points, is here strong: why a person plays in the first place (and his or her general outlook on the game as a whole) is one thing; that person's detailed obedience to the rules as such, another.

If we add the importance of reasons to what we saw earlier about the scope of discipline, we gain something which is of particular relevance to practical teaching: that is, an idea of discipline *as an educational objective in its own right* – not just as a facilitator for education. One might perhaps categorize it under moral or political education. It involves the understanding and practice of a particular virtue, confined to particular types of situation which are nevertheless of great practical importance: roughly, situations which are 'tight' enough for us to want to speak of 'discipline' as against more general terms such as 'law-abiding'. This has very little to do with notions vaguely canvassed under such headings as 'autonomy', 'self-discipline' and others, and has to be sharply separated from them.

There are reasons why this particular educational objective is important, and why it is currently in dispute. Briefly, it will appear, to liberally minded adults in a civilized, peaceful and pluralistic society, as if the number of tightly structured, quasi-military situations in which our pupils are likely to find themselves is small, and as if such situations were either not very important or positively objectionable (perhaps as leading to 'conformism' or 'authoritarianism', or whatever). Conversely, there are those who are naturally predisposed to such situations, and who will instinctively favour increasing them (one thinks here of demands to reintroduce military service, Outward Bound courses, and so on). Leaving prejudice aside, however, we need to note:

1. It is inevitable that children are born and will spend some years in a situation which is tightly structured in the way described. The family is a group of this kind: so is the classroom and the school as a whole. Notions like obedience, duties, allotted tasks, and so on, are here

inexpellable notions. If children did not grasp and act upon the principle of discipline, of obedience to established authority, they could hardly survive at all: and a proper grasp of it is an essential enablement for children to learn other things.

2. Because of this, 'discipline' – although *per se* only one subheading of the general area of contractual obligation, acting out of principle, rule-following and so forth – is inevitably a crucially important area. The family and the school necessarily form the arena of children's first encounter with the whole business of rules and authority; if children do not grasp the relevant points in this arena, it is unlikely (certain developmentalists might say, impossible) that they will do so later when they come to wider and less structured contexts in which the word 'discipline' is less applicable.

3. Although not many social groups are 'military', a great many are more like a peacetime army than they are like (say) a university or a collection of Bohemian artists. We may legitimately speak of 'discipline' in groups of people building bridges, making cars, digging coal, trawling for fish, and a large number of other cases. It is clear enough that – be our or any other society as 'liberal' as it may – we should not survive very long without adequate discipline in such contexts. And these are the contexts in which most of our pupils will in fact operate.

The contrast between discipline, in the sense outlined, and the quite different notion of being 'controlled' or 'trouble-free', is one which teachers (whether they know it or not) face every day. Not infrequently it produces a conflict of aims. Given sufficient charm, bribes, rewards, etc. – or just the willingness to overlook offences – it may be possible to keep a class of pupils trouble-free; if we insist on discipline, we may create more trouble rather than less. Many teachers are in a position where they are doing well if they can survive; it seems a bit much to ask them to take on discipline as well. If they let offenders get away with it, who shall blame them? Bribe the bully, let the tiresome child play truant, put the badly behaved out of the room if absolutely necessary, overlook the rule-breaker, turn a blind eye to the lazy and thank God for the end of term.

Together with the absence of conceptual clarity about discipline, unsurprisingly, goes the absence of any serious support for teachers in the task of enforcing and teaching discipline. Here we go back to the notion of *control*, perhaps the best word to use for the most fundamental requirements of any social group. If anything is to *be done* or not to be done – with no worries, for the moment, about reasons which people use for doing or not doing it – then there must be ways of ensuring that it is done: 'control' may stand for these ways. 'Control' may, as we have seen, operate by all sorts of methods: hypnosis, electric shocks, terror, bribery, drugs, conditioning, appeals to reason, and so on – including, of course, the straightforward use of force (as when we pick a child up and simply carry him or her to bed). Teachers must have enough methods of control at their disposal to get done what they want done or, more simply, they must have enough *power*. Without this they cannot be sure of achieving any of their objectives: and this includes the sophisticated objectives of turning out pupils who may be described (vaguely) as 'autonomous', 'rational', 'independent', 'free-thinking', 'critical' and so on. Indeed, the more sophisticated the objective, the more power and methods of control they are likely to need. It is an obvious fallacy to suppose that 'liberal' aims entail 'liberal' ('democratic' etc.) methods alone.

Important questions may be raised about the conceptual and empirical connection between methods of control and the learning of discipline: an area largely unexplored because of the naïve assumptions that they are the same thing anyway, and even if they are not, our aims and methods in both areas ought to have the same flavour – 'free', 'liberal', 'strict', or whatever the prevailing taste may be. What I want to stress here is that serious *educational* objectives, and in particular the teaching of discipline, necessarily require a great deal more control (power) than the teacher usually has available. For clearly the teacher will want to try out such things as: getting pupils to make up and obey their own rules, putting them in contexts of obedience which vary in different dimensions (different types of authority, different specific rules, different types of enforcement, different styles of obedience, etc.), clarifying and 'making real' the concepts involved not only by direct instruction but also by role-play, impromptu drama, simulated situations and so on – and no doubt the imaginative teacher will be able to think of many more practical methods.

Now this requires much more than might be meant by 'control' in some such phrase as 'keeping control' ('maintaining order', etc.). Rather, the teacher needs to be able, at the drop of a hat, to get orders carried out, to switch pupils rapidly and smoothly from one context to another, and to obtain instant participation in whatever system or rule structure s/he thinks desirable. Much of this will be a matter of getting pupils used to various structures and activities in something like the way in which a PE instructor or a teacher of impromptu dramatics often does – 'Right, now it's a dictatorship, X is dictator', 'Now you're teaching a class of five-year-olds: what rules do you make?', 'OK, I'm one of the class, I break this rule – what do you do?', and so on.

I spell this out in a naïve and long-winded way because it is essential to see that teachers need to have pupils 'in the hollow of their hand' rather than just 'in hand'. For many this is an alarming picture, generating words like 'totalitarian', 'tyranny', and so on. But it is a necessary one, and contrasts strongly with a picture of the teacher as not much more than a one-person noise abatement society. This applies, of course, to other forms of learning than learning discipline – much of moral education in general, as well as other things, will need this kind of treatment. There is a sort of vicious circle here: unless and until teachers can exercise this sort of 'control' (if we must call it that), one is tempted to say, they cannot teach pupils discipline; and cannot exercise such control fully, at least, unless and until pupils are tolerably well disciplined.

This makes it all the more important to place as much stress as possible, or at least as necessary, upon direct *obedience* to the teacher, his or her authority, and the efficiency of the sanctions required to back it up. It seems that such obedience must first be established, whatever reasons the pupil may have for obeying: on that the teacher can then build, improving the pupil's reasons and conceptual grasp. For reasons into which we need not enquire, obedience is still extremely unfashionable: the term is not often used, perhaps partly because it represents a concept less easy to avoid than what I have taken to be the central concept marked by 'discipline'.

II   AUTHORITY

Questions about 'authority' and concepts connected with it are of great practical importance for teachers. For though the individual teacher may not by him or herself be able to change the various laws and regulations which affect the job (the truancy laws, for instance, or his or her legal rights in the area of discipline and punishment), yet in practice s/he has a good deal of latitude. The teacher can try to enforce, or turn a blind eye; and more generally, his or her acceptance or rejection of particular views of 'authority' will often determine what actually goes on in schools – particularly what goes on by way of educating pupils in relation to these concepts, as we saw in the case of 'discipline'.

A set of interconnected concepts – 'authority', 'rules', 'punishment', 'institutions', and others – mark logically inevitable or inexpellable features of human social life or interaction: concepts which are bound to have *some* application or instantiation, and which it will be both senseless and unnecessary to 'challenge', 'question', or 'justify' in *general*. Thus anything that could seriously be called a 'society' or 'social group', as against a collection of hermits who happen to be living in the same area, involves some kind of interaction between its members; and 'interaction' here will not mean just that they bump up against each other like physical objects, but that they engage in some rule-following activity – even if, as perhaps in the case of a seminar or a tea-party, the activity consists only or chiefly of linguistic communication. There will therefore be rules or norms which are commonly subscribed to, whether or not they are codified, overtly agreed and stated beforehand, or contracted for. A breach of these rules must, at least characteristically if not in every case, be taken to entail the enforcement of some disadvantage on the breaker. If this were not so, we should not be able to identify them as rules prohibiting X and enjoining Y, rather than enjoining X and prohibiting Y: or else we should not be able to identify them as rules at all, as against wishes, pious hopes, generalizations about human behaviour, or descriptions of some other-worldly ideal. A social rule enjoining X exists only if, when people fail to perform X, something which is characteristically a disadvantage is normally enforced on them. Various words may be in place for the *type* of 'disadvantage' – 'punishment', 'penalty', 'sanctions' etc. – as well as for the *form* of 'disadvantage' – 'ostracism', 'imprisonment', 'exile'. Not all these disadvantages will be *painful*, but they will all be characteristically 'bad things', otherwise they would not be disadvantages but rewards.

For much the same reason two other notions (among many), generally marked by the terms 'authority' and 'institution', are also inexpellable. Any society or interacting group of rational creatures must have a common decision-procedure: indeed this can be taken as a defining characteristic of a society. We cannot conceive of a society of highly moral beings living together amicably out of respect for a moral law and for each other as rational beings, without anyone being in authority, and without anyone being thought of as an authority. The reason is not only because people are inherently non-angelic, 'bloody-minded', but because in order to *express* their amicable dispositions and have respect for each other such beings would need decision-procedures and authorities to operate them. If you cash out the notion of 'normative order' into actual cases of things that these beings might *do* – exchange goods, play hockey, hold debates, run railways, or whatever – the point becomes clear. Authorities, referees, arbitrators, umpires, etc. are necessary, not just to punish vice, but to provide clarity in those rule-governed activities: 'the editor's decision is final', not or not only because somebody has to mark down incompetent entries, but because it has to be clear what counts as winning the competition. In the same sort of way (the argument need not be put on stage again) the structural contexts which incorporate and clothe these activities – that is, 'institutions' – are also inevitable.

It may still seem as if the conceptual points made in this chapter convey no more than the bleak message 'You must obey authority'. And does this not have the very unpleasant implications marked by such phrases as 'unquestioning obedience', 'conformism', 'authoritarian regimes', and so on? Does it not lead directly to the horrors perpetrated by those who, like the Nazis, slavishly and uncritically did what they were told? How, then, can we accept these conceptual points (assuming them to be correct) whilst at the same time educating our children to think for themselves and question authority? How can it be possible both to obey and challenge?

It may seem at first sight as if the whole idea of 'questioning authority' is somehow contradictory. If one has authority, the implication is that one is and ought to be, at least characteristically, obeyed *whether or not* one's *particular* commands are thought by the individual to be wise, or pleasant, or on other grounds acceptable. Otherwise there would be no difference between an authority and an adviser. The authority of a ship's captain rests on him or her being obeyed, at least in regard to the ship's management, irrespective of the views of this or that sailor. There is one sense, therefore, in which 'unquestioning obedience' is required by the very notion of authority: just as such obedience, in certain task-like situations, constitutes part of what it is to be well disciplined. Certainly if there were too many cases of challenge or disobedience, we should hesitate to say that there was any authority (or any discipline) at all.

But this will only seem alarming and difficult if we persist in regarding 'authority' as equivalent to one particular set of power-holders or 'authorities': rather as a simple-minded person might identify 'morality' with the particular *mores* of his or her own society, or 'religion' with the particular religious beliefs and institutions with which he happened to be familiar. Of course we can question, challenge, disobey or dispense entirely with these particular manifestations: but we cannot, as I see it, hope to do without some manifestation – not, at least, so long as we remain human beings and interact socially with each other. Just as it is a conceptual truth that human beings must accept some authority and obey it if they are to get anything done, so it is also conceptually true that – if they are indeed human beings, and not robots or zombies – questions will inevitably arise about whether particular authorities are legitimate, whether their scope is properly delimited, whether the form and methods by which they operate are as good as we can make them, and so forth.

This is, or ought to be, entirely familiar ground to us. It is roughly similar to saying that, on the one hand, we must abide by whatever the rules of the game are if we are to play games at all: but that, on the other hand, we need sometimes – perhaps often – to think about what sorts of games to play, what rules it would be best to have, whether to have referees or just books of rules, and all the other matters which we need to get straight. Or, again, it is like saying that, on the one hand, there must be some sort of government (sovereign body, set of decision-makers) if we are to act together as a society at all; but that, on the other hand, we need contexts in which we can keep a watching brief on, and often revise, the form or constitution of the government, the delimitation of its sovereignty, or the particular people we want to have as decision-makers.

It is important to note that, even when we engage in this process of reconsideration and revision, we do not thereby step outside of the notion of authority altogether. If pupils in school decided to rebel against the teachers' authority, some other authority would inevitably arise: not only after the success of the rebellion, but in order to carry the rebellion through. Perhaps the pupils would meet and abide by a democratic vote; perhaps they would accept the lead of the strongest and most vociferous. But they would have to accept something.

Of course sensible societies or social groups make proper arrangements for the business of revision. Instead of allowing a free-for-all in which the strongest or most persuasive party is likely to win power, they institutionalize conflicts of opinion and desire: that is, they provide some sort of mechanism or procedure which their members agree to use – for instance, to vote rather than assassinate, or to advance arguments rather than to throw bombs. Agreement about these ultimate decision-procedures is crucial: the alternative to sincere agreement and negotiation within accepted rules being either mindless conformity, or some sort of civil war.

In educating pupils to raise questions and be critical about particular manifestations of authority, the most important thing is to provide proper contexts in which this can be done: or perhaps one should say, to allow and encourage the pupils to create and abide by contexts they themselves opt for – since it is more than half the battle to get them to see that the serious 'questioning of authority' itself involves obedience to rules. The task is to show them, or let them come to grasp, that rules and authority are logically required by human co-operation, and not simply imposed from outside in one particular form by one particular set of people (teachers, or parents, or 'society'. or whoever). Success in this task will almost certainly involve giving pupils a good deal of freedom to act out the experiences necessary to grasp the point – though not letting them go so far as the children in Golding's *Lord of the Flies* – rather than just talk about it: serious thinking tends to be promoted by having actual responsibility, and taking the consequences of one's own errors.

Are there not, though, some general principles which should guide us (and our pupils) when we are 'questioning authority' in these contexts? What sorts of reasons could we have for setting up one particular manifestation of authority (together with its attendant rules and sanctions) rather than another? Ought our regimes to be more 'democratic' or 'authoritarian', or to involve more 'participation' or 'pupil power'? As these terms suggest, there are certainly some general pressures – climates of opinion or feeling – which affect the running of educational institutions in various ways. Can we say anything sensible about all this?

The first and perhaps most important thing to be said is that any overall or *a priori* preference for a particular style or regime – 'authoritarian', 'democratic', or whatever – is likely to be doctrinaire. As our examples show, everything depends on *what sort of interaction* we want to take place: on what sort of business we want to conduct, what our particular purposes are. The style or regime suitable for an army or a ship of war will differ from that suitable for running a railway, a factory or a school. Moreover, it is clear that much depends on the people themselves: their age, or maturity, common sense or natural tendencies. Thus it would be ludicrous to attempt a 'democratic' regime for young children in wartime: first, because such children are not capable of the sort of participation required, and second because the exigencies of war demand rapid obedience to the commands of some clear-cut authority. Equally it would be ludicrous to attempt authoritarianism in a seminar for intelligent adults: first, because the adults are capable of the relevant participation, and second because anything properly called a 'seminar' could not (almost by definition) be conducted unless the participants actually participated on something like an 'egalitarian' or 'democratic' basis – if it were to be 'authoritarian' it would simply turn into a situation where the professor dictated to the students what they should think and say.

We can see, I think, that little or nothing is gained by doctrinaire preferences ('authoritarian', 'democratic', or whatever). The fact is that very often we do not know what regimes really suit what sorts of people when they conduct various kinds of business. One difficulty is that people may think that a particular regime suits them – usually one in which they are given more direct power in decision-making – but *be wrong*: not only may the regime be inefficient for conducting whatever particular business they are engaged in, but it may also make them feel unhappy, insecure and desperately anxious. Whether it really suits particular social groups to have democratic government, or young people to have complete control over their own sexual behaviour – these are, I think, very open questions which should wait on more psychological and sociological knowledge: though, of course, climates of feeling usually foreclose the questions in different ways at different times.

So far as what suits the particular clientele is concerned, teachers can only rely on their own common sense and experience assisted by whatever psychologists and others can tell us. But we can make a good deal more progress by being clear about what suits the business we are conducting. For thereby we become clear about what sorts of decisions need to be made and what sorts of authorities we need to accept and obey: what rules and sanctions are necessary for the business, and what considerations are relevant and irrelevant. Where the nature of our business is fairly obvious, we usually manage to do this: nobody would think of running an army by democratic vote, or trying to solve a mathematical problem by deferring to the Chief Constable. It is when we are less clear about what we are trying to do that we have doubts about the nature of the authority needed.

Since education is to do with the planning of serious and sustained learning, then we have at least a few obvious points to bear in mind. First, authority must be exercised to ensure that such learning can in fact take place, and to encourage it: and by the same token, we do not require authority to go beyond the purposes of learning. Thus, at least *prima facie*, the authority would have power and scope to ensure that the pupils did a minimum of work, turned up on time, did not disrupt the teaching, did not interfere with each other in such a way as to prevent each other from learning, and so on. Equally it would *not* have the power or scope to dictate, say, the pupils' dress or hair-style, unless it could be shown that these directly affected their learning. Of course this is only a very general point: a great deal will depend on *what* is to be learned and – something which follows from that – the *contexts* in which it can best be learned. Both these may be disputed. But at some stage we shall have to commit ourselves (and our pupils) to some sort of content, some set of objectives: and the important thing is to spell these out as clearly as we can. The question of authority can only be answered in that light.

Secondly, we can ensure that the authority (together with the rules and sanctions that go with it) is *clearly defined* in its scope and powers, and *properly enforced*. These are, again, obvious points, if much neglected in practice. Everybody in the business – ourselves, the pupils, their parents, and all those connected with the enterprise – needs to know just what the rules are, and what sanctions back them up; who can enforce what upon whom, by what methods, and under what circumstances. Unless this is done, those in the business will not know where they are, and if the situation is too vague, the whole existence of any authority may be called into question, with the result that what actually happens is determined by pressure groups, vociferous individuals, power-seekers, or mere inertia. It is from this sort of chaos, in which the strongest have their way and the weakest go to the wall, that the entire apparatus of authority, rules, laws, constitutions, sanctions and the rest is supposed to save us: and unless it is defended with remorseless clarity, as well as being revised and overhauled when necessary, chaos is the inevitable result.

Third, we can try (by whatever methods seem appropriate) to show our pupils that the ideal form of authority – for serious learners – really consists of the rules, procedures and standards inherent in what is being learned. Teachers and other educators act as mediators between these standards and the pupils: their job is to bring the pupils, so far as possible, to a state in which they are willing and able to pursue the subjects for their own sake – that is, to obey the demands of truth which each subject incorporates. These demands, as any serious learner well knows, are no less stringent than the orders issued by teachers and other personalized authorities: it is, again, not a matter of escaping from authority and rules altogether, but of accepting the type of authority and rules which is most nearly appropriate to the activity. The whole point of the teacher's authority is to move pupils in this direction.

III   STAFF–STUDENT CONFLICTS

Too often, in practice, a cold war, or at least some degree of coolness, is common between staff and students. Occasionally it hots up to maximum temperature, at which point a student may incarcerate him or herself in the top of a tower at an American university with a 0.50 rifle and shoot teachers on the campus. Experience persuades us that the symptoms, causes and cures are common to most or all instances of such conflicts; that the strictly intellectual aspects of the problem yield fairly easily to an elementary knowledge of moral philosophy and psychiatry; and that practice can be improved partly by such knowledge but chiefly by the willingness of both parties to own up to their own emotional states; something easier said than done.

Rational attitudes are inevitably, or at least characteristically, harder to adopt than personal or autistic attitudes simply because rational attitudes and reason in general involve shelving one's individual passions (sometimes one's individual interests) in favour of some wider and less immediately perceptible good, quelling 'the fat, relentless ego' and trying to emerge from what Plato (*Republic*, p. 315) calls 'the world of sights and sounds'.

This point is strengthened when we talk of our reactions to authority: rational or functional authority is something the growing child cannot, in principle, grasp before grasping the much more primitive concepts of authority based on naked power, or charisma of some kind, or uncritical tradition, or an ideology common to both the authorities and clients. Our early understanding and experience of these ultimately irrational or non-rational kinds of authority are, obviously enough, what conditions most of our adult behaviour towards authority in general. When a particular ideology, or set of values, or even just a set of conventions governing the etiquette of social behaviour is no longer shared, it is not surprising that we do not at once remedy the situation by the only possible method – that is, by establishing a new consensus or contractual deal.

We should be even less surprised if we are not clear about the point and scope of particular deals. The kind of rules and discipline required for the effective running of, say, an army, a hospital or a sailing ship are comparatively obvious; and there is, moreover, a fairly immediate and disastrous pay-off if we get the rules wrong – battles are lost, people die on the operating table, the ship sinks. With education this is not so. Some of our confusion is understandable; there is, indeed, room for argument (both conceptual and empirical) about just what the enterprise we mark by 'education' requires – certainly, there are borderline cases and fuzzy areas. But most of it, if understandable (for education has always been a natural arena for the play of fashion, fantasy and metaphysics), is certainly not justifiable. If somebody were to say, for instance, that it does not matter for education whether or not students work as they are told, whether teachers have the power to enforce the discipline necessary for the work to be done, if buildings necessary for the work were occupied or, conversely, that it does very much matter for education whether or not students wear beards, or are homosexual or chew gum, then, in default of some sound argument to the contrary (and there may, of course, always be such an argument), one would claim that they have an insecure grasp of the concept of education. They do not understand what education is or is for. They have confused the enterprise with other enterprises of a moral, aesthetic or ideological nature.

Such confusion is, in fact, very common. It is one thing to argue for school uniform, certain styles of dress and language or sexual behaviour on moral or aesthetic grounds, quite another to argue for them on educational grounds. The tendency to introduce our own, or our society's, ideological preferences into education shows how tenuous our desire to educate really is. We are much more concerned to defend or impose our own values. It is not, in fact, very difficult to list those rules that are necessary to, say, the proper running of a university, a college or a school, provided we stick to educational criteria; naturally, as soon as politics, or morality, or any sort of personal ideal is allowed a free hand, there is no limit to conflict and no secure area of co-operation. The position is like one in which two individuals or corporations refuse to trade with, say good morning to or play games with each other because each believes that the other has the wrong religion, skin colour or political beliefs. Of course, nobody (in their right senses) would actually prescribe a general principle by which anyone was permitted to interrupt functional enterprises for ideological reasons, but then we do not often achieve the detachment needed to think about the issue in a reasonable manner. We prefer to strike out and make gestures when we can.

When consensus breaks down and there is no contract to replace it, the symptoms are predictable and painful. It is not so much that the various parties are clear-headed about identifying and negotiating their particular interests in a reasonable way; that would pretty rapidly lead to a new deal. It is rather that they strike attitudes and stand on their dignity, the only thing they can cling to if they are to avoid the more extreme feelings of chaos. Gangs labelled 'we' and 'they' are rapidly formed; almost any point, however reasonably advanced, is taken personally; communications become increasingly stylized and less informal; and before you know where you are, an issue that could easily be settled in ten minutes over a glass of sherry by a small group of reasonable people fails to be settled by lengthy and arduous meetings of joint committees and by the formal interchange of innumerable pieces of paper. The whole scene becomes at once tragic and laughable: it is above all an unreal scene, a kind of play-acting or mime in which the agents act out their parts in a dream-like way.

Equally classical and reminiscent of early childhood are the symptoms peculiar to each party. The students, perceiving the uncertainty of the authorities, test their limits out (sometimes virtually to the point of destruction), like young children gauging how much they can get away with. Whether or not the actual issues have real importance (and of course, they may), they test for the sake of testing rather than for the sake of the issues – or, rather, for the sake of seeing where they stand and what norms are actually in force. They may do this half playfully, or more anxiously and hence more ferociously. The staff, lacking the confidence of ideological commitment and having no alternative rationale on which to rely, at once feel threatened. They have nothing to stand between them and chaos except the orthodox liberal hope that the students want to be reasonable and will become so if they treat them more as equals or make various moves under such headings as 'democracy' or 'participation'. They entertain the fantasy that patience, calm persuasion, clear argument and impersonal adjudication will eventually win the day, though this does not always prevent them from feeling personally attacked and alarmed. In general, they are less clear about whether they should be acting as parents, elder siblings or equals than the students are about acting as rebellious children, so that the tendency is for the students to gain ground rather than to lose it.

It is important to appreciate that the amount of rational thinking that goes on is much less than either party consciously admits to. What is at stake is a number of highly generalized pictures to which each side is wedded and which become much sharper and painted in much more lurid colours as the conflict continues. Much of what is done and said is symbolic rather than conceived in terms of cause and effect (rather as, in some quarters, independent schools are hated as symbols of 'divisiveness', whether or not they actually cause it). On one side, staff object to long hair, bad language, certain styles of dress and whatever seems to them contrary to a generalized picture of the 'good' student: on the other, there is considerable student resentment of the particular privileges enjoyed by staff that seem to flaunt their authority or status – having separate common rooms and so forth. Gestures are often symbolic, in that they often have no logical connection with the point of dispute.

But it does not follow from this that the phenomena must be seen only in the light of some totally non-rational malaise or social disease, not to be negotiated by reason. This leads to the idea that our best bet is to keep a low profile and by some means to 'avoid trouble' if we are the authorities or that we should keep up some form of pressure if we are the students. Governments characteristically behave like this, paying Danegeld to any potential troublemakers (the praetorian guard, the trades unions or businesses with muscle) in order simply to buy them off, without reference to justice or contract. We even prefer to cancel football matches or to prevent some people from attending, rather than allow them to attend while ensuring that sufficiently clear and strong rules and sanctions will operate to make them behave properly. There are, of course, devices that authorities can use to inhibit student unrest and devices that students can use (mostly involving collective action) to wear down the staff, but these are irrelevant. They relate to particular fears or desires for particular troubles, not to establishing long-term mechanisms for dealing with potential trouble in general.

There are two types of cure for these conflicts, both fairly obvious and necessary and to be applied simultaneously. The important thing is to distinguish them.

The more obvious of the two is the establishment of clear, detailed, agreed and enforceable contracts in advance of conflict. Many people dislike the very idea of this, preferring to rely on some general (if non-existent) consensus about what is 'reasonable' or 'decent'. At one institution much that should have been determined by clear rules was, in fact, adjudicated in terms of 'reasonable behaviour'; predictably, what the students regarded as reasonable behaviour was wildly different from what the staff envisaged. Naturally, not everything can be spelled out in terms of rules; but a great deal can, and what is left can be stated to reside within the authority of this or that body or individual. Only then can both sides know what the rules of the game actually are and what is to happen if someone breaks them. Any space left outside the rules is always potentially space for conflict (as, indeed, we see in actual games: it is precisely the absence of rules about behaviour on the tennis court, for instance, that allows the wearisome scenes now so common at tournaments to take place).

Contracts must satisfy four criteria: they must be fair, agreed, clear and enforced. Of these, the most difficult in principle is the first, but in educational matters the difficulty is much diminished. For either (in schools) we regard the clients as minors, which allows the authorities (the educators themselves or other social agencies) to frame the contracts in the light of their own unilateral judgement, though bearing in mind the best interests of the clients, or else (in higher education) the institution is selective – like members of a club, the clients do not have to join and need not sign up if they do not want to. There is no reason against, and many reasons for, allowing different institutions to offer quite a wide variety of different contracts, though of course, since they are all concerned with education, there will be much common ground.

That the contracts should be agreed – and that means, crucially, agreed and signed in advance – is straightforward enough, though it is extremely important that all clients should understand, before signing, exactly what rules they are subscribing to and exactly what sanctions will apply if they break them. That is a matter of making the contract clear rather than attempting to rely on 'good sense', 'goodwill' or anything of that kind. There is no harm in spelling out even obvious details: if goodwill is present anyway, nothing is lost; and if it is not, a great deal of time and energy is saved. Nor is enforcement particularly problematic, particularly since many institutions have the option of simply dismissing any clients who will not play by the rules – an option, we think, that all educational institutions should enjoy (even where education is compulsory), since there is a sharp limit to the desirability of educating a person against his or her will.

We give here simply the most obvious elements of the formal framework, since we believe the clarity and firmness of that framework to be more important than the particular content – extreme and improbable cases excepted, of course – just as, apart from cases of gross over-severity or laxness, it is much more important for a growing child to have a clear set of parental rules within which to live than for those rules to be of this or that kind. Naturally, this does not mean that contracts cannot be more or less sensible in content. But there are two general guidelines to help us here. First, there is the criterion or set of criteria offered by the enterprise of education itself, which is what the whole apparatus is for: this we have mentioned already. Secondly there are principles of natural justice that can steer us away from the purely symbolic or ideological. In fact, these latter are often disregarded: for instance, it seems clearly just that one who causes damage to another should be expected to compensate the victim for whatever damage one has done (that might, indeed, reasonably be taken as the root idea of retribution), so that fixed or token fines appear not to fit such cases. That is perhaps only one rather obvious illustration of the way in which types of sanctions or enforcement have become ritualized or disconnected from the purposes which they serve.

Nor, of course, do we claim that educational institutions are sovereign states: they are given parameters within which to work by other institutions and by society at large. They also have to pay considerable attention to public relations. Just how much attention depends on many variables, one of the most important being the extent to which educators are themselves prepared to be clear about how much power they need in order to educate and to be willing to fight for it. But this really makes no difference to the formal framework: if certain rules have to be written in for the benefit of public relations rather than on strictly educational grounds, so be it. As long as the rules are clear and their rationale is honestly described, they can legitimately form part of the deal.

All this allows the administration to operate impersonally, without much or any argument; and there are, as we have already hinted, deep psychological reasons why the idea is resisted – apart, that is, from the mere naïvety of failing to distinguish this cure from the procedures represented below, which are to do with establishing trust and good communications in general. Liberals as well as anarchists dislike the idea of rules, usually picturing them as restrictive or pedantic rather than enabling (as they also are). Part of the alarm here is the relinquishing of personal wants and judgements to impersonal procedures: rules are seen as 'dehumanizing' (as if the rules of tennis somehow 'dehumanized' the game), even if we build into the rules – as naturally we shall – second-order principles about legitimate methods of changing them. They are felt to inhibit fraternity, as if genuine fraternity itself did not rely on adherence to rules – as if, indeed, it did not partly consist of such adherence. But the main fear, we believe, is fear of separation, particularly on the part of the authorities. In giving orders or enforcing impersonal rules we distance ourselves, if only for a time, from children, students or other clients. We are no longer (we feel) loved or even respected for ourselves, and in the absence of a sustaining and legitimizing authority, we feel isolated and unsupported. Liberals, one might say, so much want to be friends with their children and they dislike the idea of authority altogether and unconsciously welcome any confusion that masks its essence.

The second cure consists, again very obviously, of a serious attempt to engender trust and communication. Though both cures need to be operated, it is very important to preserve a clear distinction between the two. Without that, and without seeing the point of each, we relapse into a disastrous style of thinking along a certain dimension marked perhaps by 'tough-minded' at one end of the scale and 'tender-minded' at the other. (Thus we feel that we ought to be a bit tough on criminals in prison because, after all, they are criminals; then again we feel that we ought not to be too tough because, after all, we are kind people; so we occupy a kind of muddled middle position.) It is not a matter of trying to adjust a balance, a judicious admixture of tough rule-making and enforcing, and tender communication and kindness: it is a matter of operating two different and parallel enterprises. It is one thing to act as an authority, another to act as an equal. Nothing is gained, and a lot lost, by adopting any kind of half-and-half position.

Trust and communication take time to produce. Among the things that accelerate them, formal procedures and most of what goes on under the heading of 'participation' are not numbered. Efficient methods are necessarily informal; they are also likely to be simple in content – eating and drinking together, playing games together, engaging in joint tasks that stress what is common to both parties rather than the peculiar tastes or expertise of either.

It will be evident that these procedures are far removed not only from political participation but also from most of what goes on under clinical headings like 'pastoral care' and 'counselling'. Even our own phraseology – 'procedures' for 'engendering trust' – is dangerous: what is required, quite simply, is that at least some members of staff should actually like being with their students in an informal context and that the students should like it too. This involves the requirements that the institution should appoint people on that principle and should recognize the job (another dangerous term) as an essential one. It is not everybody's cup of tea: perhaps the most serious difficulty in education is how to get enough people of the right sort. The reason why we have to take it seriously, which is also the reason why it is apt to become over-stylized and clinical, is simply that this kind of informal interaction is in very short supply. The reasons for this in turn are various. Some are simple, such as shortage of time and pressure of work; others, however, are fantasy-based, one predominant fantasy being that the students do not need it and/or do not want it. Of these the first is always false and the latter usually false. Any serious or genuine education depends on a kind of parenting. The idea that young people, or indeed people of almost any age, are able and willing to engage in serious and sustained learning without a supporting background of this kind seems to us extremely simple-minded.

We have so far failed to distinguish, under this general heading, contexts of interaction that are (1) egalitarian or (2) patronizing. (Both these pieces of terminology are odious: almost any terminology is.) We mean simply that there will naturally be times when the two parties meet as equals (most obviously, for instance, when drinking, or talking, or playing some kind of game together on neutral ground) and other times when one entertains the other (as it were on home ground). Both are important for both parties, allowing everyone the opportunity to forget all about temporary or permanent differences of status on the one hand and, on the other, to patronize or be patronized. One advantage of the former is that contexts may be chosen – a suitable kind of game, for example – that permit the natural talents of youth to outshine those of the staff: in the latter case, it is perhaps particularly important that the students should be expected and encouraged to invite staff into the students' territory, which puts the students temporarily into a position of power. (One of the awful things about being educated is that people are always doing something to you, whether nice or nasty. An occasional reversal of this general role is extremely desirable.)

More problematic because of the dangers of clinical formality, but in our judgement worth trying if supported by other less formal contexts, is the even more direct method of holding seminars or working groups designed to encourage the necessary insight. However much one's temperament may react against the more extravagant or, as it were, Californian versions of encounter groups and other therapy groups, it seems feeble-minded or intellectually dishonest not to make some such attempt. The alternative is simply to allow each side to go on thinking dark thoughts (and some of them are unbelievably dark) about the other but never to have these expressed in any joint context. In general, the more intellectually sophisticated the institution, the stronger the mental defences against attempting any such thing: we preserve the pretence that all or most of us, students as well as staff, are too level-headed or sensible to require such treatment or, alternatively, that it is not our business. Anyone who does not perceive the element of fantasy here is unlikely to be persuaded by anything that we write.

Chapter 9

PSE and moral education

There is a whole area of education which is concerned with the pupil's character, morality, emotions, and way of life, both as an individual and as a member of society. It is obviously an area of immense importance, but there is much dispute about it. This dispute shows itself even in the titles used to describe it. Currently, in many British schools, 'personal and social education' (PSE) is the preferred title; though 'citizenship' and numerous other titles have been used. I have chosen 'moral education' for this chapter and 'pastoral care' for the next because these seem to cover the ground best; but that itself is disputable, and the whole question of how to delimit and perhaps subdivide the area needs further discussion.

What is not (I hope) in dispute, however, is that this area is fundamentally concerned with *values*, not just with facts; and it is absolutely essential to consider the logical basis of any education in the area of moral and other values – that is, the basis of moral education. This will be our starting-point.

I UNDERSTANDING THE BASIS

This is by far the most important requirement, because without it nothing serious can be done, however much money and effort are deployed. Moral education requires (a) a *non-partisan* approach: that is, an approach derived from pure reason and not from the tenets of any particular creed, culture, ideology or set of 'social values'. As with any other subject or department of life, we have to grasp what counts as 'a good performer in the moral sphere' and list the attributes of such a performer; this has nothing much to do with 'society' or 'a general consensus', but with coming to understand what we would mean by 'being reasonable' or 'being educated' in this area. We have to list these attributes, and show that reason requires each of them, otherwise we are not educating, but merely selling some kind of party line. However, education requires also (b) a *methodology*: that is, although we do not sell the pupils our own right answers just because they are our own, we do initiate them into *how* to *get* right answers and how to act on them effectively. Again as with any other educational subject, we show pupils what sort of reasons are appropriate, what kinds of procedures and qualities they need to do the subject properly. Without this, we should not be educating them at all: there would be no principles of reason to educate them in, and we should merely be giving them scope to 'discuss' or be 'stimulating concern' about moral matters without any suggestions that there were such things as right and wrong answers, wise or unwise decisions, relevant or irrelevant considerations, sane or insane views. (Many current projects do not do much more than this.)

It is worth noting that these points apply to other educational titles that may be preferred to 'moral education', or that overlap with it; for instance, 'social education', 'value education', 'political education', or titles of a still vaguer kind – 'learning to live', 'learning to grow up', 'education in personal relationships', and so forth. I mention this because it seems remarkably difficult for people to grasp the two basic points, (a) and (b) in the previous paragraph, under any heading whatsoever. If one asks, for example, what 'political education' is supposed to consist of, the answer given in some circles is roughly:

> Pupils ought to know how their political system works (the details of government, the party system, etc.); of course they ought not to be indoctrinated with the views of any one party, but they ought to learn how to play a full part in a democratic system.

That sort of line is demonstrably feeble-minded: for (1) it may be bad to have a 'democratic system' (whatever that may mean) – Plato thought so, and pupils should at least realize that the matter is controversial; simply to assume that democracy is good because it is (supposedly) in force in some societies is, in fact, a kind of oblique indoctrination; (2) perhaps the 'political system' as we have it is in a high degree irrational, so that a sensible pupil might see its details as intrinsically boring; and (3) no indication is given of how pupils can be encouraged to make up their minds *rationally* on political issues – yet that, and that alone, would justify any programme seriously aimed at educating pupils *in* (not just *about*) politics.

So with other titles. We may conduct 'religious education' on some assumption, such that religion is a good thing or that there is a purpose to the universe: 'education in personal relationships' on the assumption, for instance, that people ought to get married or to be gentle in their love-making; 'social education' on the assumption that our particular society, or western society, or some 'consensus' drawn from most societies, incorporates the right values – but that gives no rational grounds for the pupils' assent (or, indeed, for our own beliefs); and sooner or later some pupils at least are going to challenge these assumptions. Indeed this happens already. If education is possible in any or all of these (overlapping) areas, it can only be so if we confront the task of working out what can reasonably count as a good (competent, perceptive, sane, etc.) decision-maker and agent in these spheres: if we have some clear idea of what reasons are relevant to them, and what personal qualities necessary. Without that, without any kind of methodology, all we can do is to swap prejudices or stick to the discussion of non-controversial facts; just as, if we did not know how to educate pupils in science, all we could do would be to tell them *about* science (about the history of science, its importance in the modern world, and so on), and let them generate their own scientific beliefs unchecked by any rational methodology.

So either:

1. We have some idea of how to get right answers to moral questions – some notion of what counts as a good reason and what does not, perhaps something approaching a methodology,

or,

2. we do not (maybe we think 'it's all relative', or maybe we are just muddled about what good reasons are in morality).

If (2), we have no right to be in the moral education business at all; thus if a pupil says 'I'm going to beat her up because it's Tuesday/because I hate her/because she's black', or whatever reason you like, all we can say is 'Ah, well, that's a point of view'. Certainly *discussion* would be useless; for serious discussion presupposes the possibility of progress via relevant reasoning, of getting nearer to right answers or truth – otherwise we are just swapping feelings. Nor would we feel we had the right to know what sort of examples to set, inspiration to give, etc. since (on this view) we have no clue as to what can fairly count as a *good* example.

I do not think anyone seriously believes (2). We have *some* idea how to do the subject, *some* grasp of what can fairly or *intelligibly* count as a reason, and of what we are committed to by the use of words like 'ought', 'right', etc. I think, of course, that we have a pretty good idea; that, at least on reflection, most sane people would accept that reasons – to count as good reasons – would have to be shown to relate to human needs and interests (rather than what some 'authority' says, or what one's inner feelings suggest to one, or what one selfishly wants, or what day of the week it is). If so, quite a lot follows: we need whatever skills, knowledge, abilities, aptitudes etc. will best enable us to work out these reasons properly and act on them. My point is simply that if we do not have any rational agreement on moral methodology and reasoning, we are not in business at all: but in so far as we do, we ought to teach it to pupils.

One might add to this basic point in three ways, defending the placing of 'moral thinking' (or whatever we want to call it) in the curriculum:

1. It is *honest*. If we suppose that we are in a position to educate pupils morally at all, then we thereby claim to have some idea about the aims of moral education, about the qualities required by people for settling moral problems reasonably and acting on their decisions. That is, we claim some knowledge of morality as a subject. If so, how can we not put this before our pupils in some form without dishonesty? Why conceal this from them?

2. It is *professional*. By this I mean that we ought to, and now can, get well beyond the stage of merely 'discussing moral problems', 'arousing concern', 'stimulating interest', 'being open-ended', and so on. A lot of (no doubt useful) work has been done along these lines; but we must give our pupils a clear idea that there are *right and wrong answers* to moral questions, that there is a coherent *methodology* for settling them. We cannot encourage the feeling expressed in such words as 'It's all relative really, isn't it?', 'It's just a matter of how you feel', 'It's a matter of taste', etc. Just as, in science or other subjects, it is one thing to encourage and help pupils to find out the answers and the reasons behind them, but quite another to imply that there are no answers; so in morality, although we do not impose our individual views as right, we must not imply that one view is as good as another.

3. It *gives the pupils something to hang on to*. I avoid here words like 'ideal', 'creed', 'faith', etc. because we are not out to give them any specific or partisan set of moral or metaphysical beliefs. What we are trying to give them is something far more important, for which 'methodology' is as good a word as I can think of. We are giving them the tools to do the job for themselves (which is the only way you can do morality anyway). Without these tools there is bound to be the 'moral vacuum' ('alienation', anxiety, sense of being lost, 'drifting', or whatever we care to call it) that many people have talked about. The tools are not intellectually very complex: the concepts and reasoning required are well within the cognitive grasp of quite young children.

What then are these tools? What are the bits of equipment which pupils (and indeed all of us) need in order to count as morally educated? Very briefly, they are (a) a recognition that other people count equally with ourselves, (b) an awareness of their and our own emotions and feelings, (c) awareness of the hard facts relevant to decision-making, (d) the ability and willingness to put (a)–(c) together and make a practical decision – that is, the alertness, patience, determination and so forth required to translate our thinking into action. These form the constituents of moral education; and its aims are, quite simply, to improve these constituents or bits of equipment so that we can think and act more reasonably in the area of morality. I have given a full list of these moral components or constituents at the end of this chapter. What teachers have to do is to grasp each component firmly, and use whatever methods (in the classroom and out of it) they think will encourage and enlarge them in their pupils. Teachers themselves will best be able to judge this; but the few points that follow may be helpful.

II   MATERIALS FOR DECISION-MAKING

Following most directly from the above, and whatever else may be needed for moral education, the teacher needs to have some coherent material on 'moral methodology' (to give it a grand name): that is, those concepts, procedures, types of reasons, abilities and so on which are basic to the subject. These come from the list of 'moral components' – that is, they include the various concepts and principles involved in concern for people (PHIL), awareness of emotions (EMP), factual knowledge and 'know-how' (GIG), and alertness and determination (KRAT). I do not here want to argue for these in detail, but I shall assume that the material in question attempts the task of explaining what is required for moral thought and action, in a quite straightforward and thorough manner, and that the teacher using it at least thinks that this is a possible and important thing to do.

I am not aware that any satisfactory material of this kind has been produced. A vast quantity has been produced, both in the UK and (even more) on the other side of the Atlantic, with apparently different aims: to stimulate thought about social or personal problems, discuss controversial issues, arouse general interest in 'values', and so on. These appear often under vague or trendy headings, like 'values clarification', 'personal development', 'learning to live', 'society today', etc. Much of this may, for various purposes, be extremely useful. But it seems fairly clear that it fights shy of the whole notion of a rational methodology, and (to say the least) does not stress the point that there are right and wrong, rational and irrational, serious and non-serious ways of making up one's mind about moral issues. The popularity of controversial issues, and of the large scale 'social' issues (pollution, war, etc.), suggest this strongly.

Issues of this kind of course exist, and are important, but they are clearly not easy to settle. To *begin* with issues of this kind seems an absurd policy for anyone who is really trying to initiate pupils into a particular methodology or form of thought. Much more naturally, as in other subjects, we should begin with clear cases of a non-controversial kind, where we have something like certain knowledge; also, with cases which are simple and nearest to the pupils' own experiences – the behaviour of one pupil or family-member to another, for instance, rather than the wider problems of politics and society. Moral education, like charity, begins at home; and a good deal of contemporary material seems evasive in more than one way.

III   METHODS

Here are a number of general methods which will occur to the teacher:

1. Going through the material point by point, giving examples in class and asking the children questions about it.
2. Encouraging the children to use sources which illustrate the material, and to bring their own examples and material (newspaper cuttings, cartoons, etc.) to the classroom.
3. Oral discussion on moral questions to which the material is relevant.
4. Oral discussion with the teacher about their emotions and personal relationships.
5. The use of videos and other visual media.
6. Acting, drama and role-playing.
7. Making a tape or videotape recording of the children's discussions, or their actual behaviour, and playing it back to them afterwards for further consideration.
8. Putting them in 'simulation situations' where they have to solve personal and moral problems.
9. Giving them experience of people unlike themselves (people of different cultural backgrounds, old people, etc.) to enlarge their understanding.
10. Getting them to make up their own rules, or organize something inside or outside the school on their own responsibility.

The reader will notice that these methods are arranged in a particular order, along a scale which might be (rather inadequately) labelled 'abstract' at one end, and something like 'concrete' or 'real-life' at the other. Method (1), the direct explanation of the material, may be 'abstract' and 'unreal' for some pupils; in method (10), on the other hand, the pupils are more or less forced to think and act for themselves. Videos and other visual aids (5) produce more personal involvement, for some pupils, than most types of discussion (3) and (4), but not so much as role-playing (6).

Rather than just picking one or two methods to support the material, teachers should ideally try to get a proper 'mix' of methods, and make sure that they are not spending too much time at one end of the scale or the other – that they are not being too 'abstract', or too 'concrete'. It will be best if they try to use a number of methods which cover the whole scale. For instance, if the teacher is dealing with concern for others (PHIL), s/he might start by going through the material (1), get the pupils to do some role-playing which illustrates PHIL (6), refer back to the material (1), tape-record their behaviour and their talk in some PHIL-type situation, such as when a stranger or a new pupil appears, and get them to discuss the recording (7), back to the material again (1), and then get them to engage in a 'real-life' experience (making up their own rules about strangers or new pupils, or getting them to help old people in the area, or whatever)

(10), and finally back to the material (1). By such a judicious mixture of 'abstract' and 'concrete' methods, the principle of PHIL may be firmly grasped. Naturally the proper 'mix' depends on the type of pupils, but almost all pupils will need supporting methods which run throughout the scale. Both 'abstract' methods and 'experience' are impotent by themselves. They have to be correlated.

Of course, social context in the school (the conditions under which the pupils learn) is equally vital. I put some suggestions here very briefly.

1. Making sure that the concept of moral education is properly understood, and that the task of moral education is responsibly undertaken.
2. Making whatever basic arrangements are necessary to bring the pupils into communication with the educators.
3. Making sure that the 'ground rules' of the institution are (a) based on the right sort of criteria (even if there is uncertainty about the facts), and (b) firmly enforced.
4. Making the rules, and the point of the rules, as clear as possible to the pupils.
5. Giving the pupils some degree of self-government, and establishing close communication in rule-making and rule-following.
6. The structuring of pastoral care in smaller groups (e.g. a house system).
7. Providing contexts which will significantly occupy the institution as a whole (e.g. some construction enterprise, mass camping or exploring, dancing, singing etc.)
8. Arranging some criteria of success in the institution, in so far as some competition is inevitable (and perhaps desirable) so that everyone succeeds in something and acquires some prestige and self-confidence thereby.
9. Arranging that there is some one person (e.g. the head teacher) who acts as the ultimate authority (at least in a psychological sense, so far as the children are concerned); and who is actually on the premises, and visibly concerned with the day-to-day running of the school.
10. Making the significant teaching unit a small group, with the same 'teacher' or adult group-leader, perhaps over a period of years, with whom the pupils can form a close personal relationship; and fitting 'specialist' or subject teaching as far as possible into this framework.
11. Opportunities to 'patronize' and feel needed, i.e. to be responsible for and of service to younger children, old people, the poor, the lonely, animals, etc.
12. Use of practical 'order and command' contexts, to see the point of discipline relevant to particular situations (e.g. in sailing, mountaineering, building and other operations with highly specific goals).

IV   OTHER MODES OF THOUGHT

The moral thinking of many pupils (and adults) is not done in terms of other people's interests at all, but in some other mode. Which mode affects particular pupils will depend on the stage of their development, and many other factors.

It may be:

1. the *'other-obeying'* mode, in which some external person, group of people, or code is taken as the ultimate authority on what to do. The 'other' may be the pupils' parents, or friends, or 'what fashion says', or the Bible, or almost anything.
2. the *'self-obeying'* mode, in which some internal feeling on the part of pupils determines what they thinks they ought to do. This may be guilt, or shame ('conscience') or perhaps some ideal that they are wedded to.
3. the *'self-considering'* mode, in which some straightforward or selfish advantage dictates pupils' thinking (they will get a reward, be detected and punished, be praised, make more money, etc.).

There is, of course, much more to be said about the kinds of mistakes mentioned above, and in particular about the kinds of emotions that engender them. Certainly the more teachers are concerned with getting pupils not just to understand the right way to 'do morality' – though this would be no mean achievement – but to be serious about applying it to their own case, the more they will find themselves forced to enter the area of education of the emotions. For it is other emotional pulls, pulls which have little to do with the attitudes of concern (PHIL) which should operate in us, that distract us all from correct moral behaviour – and sometimes go so far as to distract us from correct moral thinking.

FULL LIST OF MORAL COMPONENTS

PHIL (HC)	Having the concept of a 'person'.
PHIL (CC)	Claiming to use this concept in an overriding, prescriptive, universalized (O, P and U) principle.
PHIL (RSF)	Having feelings which support this principle, either of a
(DO & PO)	'duty-oriented' (DO) or a 'person-oriented' (PO) kind.
EMP (HC)	Having the concepts of various emotions (moods, etc.).
EMP (1) (Cs)	Being able, in practice, to identify emotions, etc. in oneself, when these are at a conscious level.
EMP (1) (Ucs)	Ditto, when the emotions are at an unconscious level.
EMP (2) (Cs)	Ditto, in other people, when at a conscious level.
EMP (2) (Ucs)	Ditto, when at an unconscious level.
GIG (1) (KF)	Knowing other ('hard') facts relevant to moral decisions.
GIG(1) (KS)	Knowing sources of facts (where to find out) as above.

GIG(2) (VC)	'Knowing how': a 'skill' element in dealing with moral situations, as evinced in verbal communication with others.
GIG(2) (NVC)	Ditto, in non-verbal communication.
KRAT(1) (RA)	Being in practice, 'relevantly alert' to (noticing) moral situations, and seeing them as such (describing them in terms of PHIL, etc. above).
KRAT(1) (TT)	Thinking thoroughly about such situations, and bringing to bear whatever PHIL, EMP and GIG one has.
KRAT(1) (OPU)	As a result of the foregoing, making an overriding, prescriptive and universalized decision to act in others' interests.
KRAT (2)	Being sufficiently whole-hearted, free from unconscious counter-motivation, etc. to carry out (when able) the above decision in practice.

Chapter 10

Pastoral care

First steps in any area of education are a matter of getting a clear idea of the general outline and nature of the particular enterprise. A list of 'aims and objectives' is often vacuous: 'enrichment', 'care', 'concern for the individual pupil', 'development of potential', etc. – nobody is going to be *against* these because they are too general for anybody to argue with. At the other end of the scale, questions like 'How long should tutorial periods be for Year 11 girls in a comprehensive school?' cannot be answered until we have a better idea of just what *sort* of thing we are trying to do under the heading of 'pastoral care'.

The title itself, like many educational titles ('creativity', 'autonomy', etc.), has to be critically inspected, because it may carry a certain set of values or foreclose certain options which, on reflection, we may want to question. 'Pastoral care' may suggest a tender-minded rather than a tough-minded approach (rather as if pupils were a kind of sheep or threatened species of wildlife); and may become separated from areas that must surely be intimately connected with it – discipline, rule-keeping, the ethos of the school, moral education and others. As so often in education, most of the crucial decisions have to do with the concepts and values with which we start, which we bring (often unconsciously) to the area. How are we to become more critical and clear about these?

One danger is a failure to confront our own prejudices sharply enough; here we shall try to list some of these. Of course not everyone shares them; and some, when stated, may be denied even by those of us who continue to operate on them in practice. Nor are we arguing here that they are all false or inadequate or misguided. But they exist, as it were, at the roots of much practice and many tacit assumptions in schools today: and they need to be questioned. These are at least some of the ideas:

1. That schools have basically to be structured round the idea of *classroom periods*: hence that pastoral care is a matter of allocating time in

classrooms with some new content, perhaps new materials.
2. That pastoral care is essentially care for particular *individuals*, not for groups of individuals working together.
3. That schools should not be *separated* from the local community, but somehow integrated with it or at least open to it as much as possible.
4. That teachers have *enough power*, scope and authority to do most of what is needed by way of changing the attitudes, emotions, character and confidence of pupils.
5. That *day schools* are at a severe disadvantage when compared with boarding schools.
6. That *older pupils* either cannot or should not be heavily relied on to control and help younger pupils.
7. That learning normally done in *classrooms* (English, RE, music, and many other subjects) can be effective without the backing of a group or community which is not based in the classroom.

Rather than argue in detail against any of these, we may usefully consider the 'pastoral care' (though already the term looks a bit odd) that operates in a satisfactory extended family. In such a context a great deal of learning goes on; and if teachers are genuinely to be *in loco parentis* – something surely required for any serious pastoral care – it is worth seeing how it is that such families do the job. Contrast with 1–7 above the following points:

(i)   Families are not based on the idea of 'periods' at all, but upon a quite different kind of structure. *They share all sorts of things* which bind their members together: common parents, common meals, outings, games, rules of conduct, discussions, work, holidays and many other things. They have (to put it briefly) shared space and shared inter-action. A family whose parents simply *talked* with each child a few times a week would be absurd: any successful talk that goes on must have this background of shared activity.

(ii) Families often work collectively, not as isolated individuals. They have common aims and activities, and do not split themselves up by age for anything like all their time.

(iii) Families are (to use the jargon) vertically rather than horizontally structured; the older children not only help the younger (and vice versa) but often exercise great psychological influence on them. Relationships of love, affection, friendship, and also discipline and control, between young and old are essential.

(iv) Whilst, of course, members of the family go into the outside world, they nevertheless have a *home*, a psychological base, which is *separated* from it and helps to protect them sometimes in the teeth of a hostile environment. The family has *its own* values and base, and does not simply copy or integrate with those of the outside world.

(v)   The parents of the family have *very great power*: power no doubt sometimes abused, but quite essential not only for control but also for care.

(vi) In families a great deal even of 'academic' learning goes on: not just in that parents may teach children to read and write, but in that the family forms a community with certain *interests* – football, music, word-games, decoration and art, or whatever. It is from this background that children pick up not only the motivation for learning but information and skills.

These points may bring out what we take to be the central question for teachers concerned with pastoral care. To put the question as sharply as possible: are we going to be *serious* about pastoral care, trying to make up for bad family experiences that our pupils may have had, and trying to give the child a genuine 'home from home' in the school, a proper psychological base (not just the classroom); or are we just going to add a few tutorial periods or pieces of counselling, a few bureaucratic ideas about 'houses' or 'tutor groups', and vaguely hope that these arrangements will really change things? Many of our pupils are desperately in need – not just those who happen to be disruptive in the classroom, or obviously disturbed. Indeed any serious educator appreciates that all of us have important psychological needs which are not (and could not conceivably be) adequately catered for by anything which would naturally happen in the *classroom*. We run a system based on the assumption that pupils come from solid, reliable extended families, and a society in which solid, reliable values prevail – so that they need only the rather more sophisticated kind of classroom-learning that families cannot give: but that assumption is plainly false. They live in a chaotic and disrupted world, and desperately need the sort of 'home from home' that they will find in the street gangs if we cannot give it to them in school.

We are suggesting, then, that effective pastoral care involves a major restructuring of the school. The most natural terminology here is that of a 'house system': but that will exist only on paper without the binding forces mentioned above – shared space, shared food and drink, shared activities, and all the rest. Naturally this involves giving considerable powers to the teachers responsible for the houses and to the house monitors (prefects, or whatever). In effect, we have to create a whole parallel system to the system of classrooms and subject departments; and that first system must be *more*, not less, powerful in social and psychological terms.

It is worth asking why (since many people, on reflection, agree with this in principle) it is not more widely adopted. Two reasons at once present themselves. First, there is a curiously large gulf between the independent schools – many of which have been running this sort of system for many years – and the state sector, with faults on both sides and a deep distrust preventing effective communication. Clearly a 'family' ('house') system of this kind cannot be regarded as a preserve for those pupils whose parents are rich enough to send them to independent schools; and we can adopt the general format or structure which they use without adopting public-school norms and values. Experience of what actually happens in good independent schools would probably be more valuable for state-school teachers than any amount of literature or discussion; at least it would clear away some prejudices. Secondly, teachers tend to see pastoral care as an added burden on their time and energies. But (see vi above) we should question whether it is necessary, or even desirable, to drive children into classrooms in a succession of periods throughout the school day. Much may be learned – we would guess, more effectively learned – within the non-academic house system; and we could cut down the number of curriculum teaching periods without serious loss.

But behind these and other more surface reasons lies, we suggest, a certain ambivalence about the idea of teachers *in loco parentis*. On the one hand, we pay lip-service to this ('care', 'concern', etc.) and would all happily assent to the statements that education is of the whole person, not just learning 'subjects', that the pupil's own emotions, confidence, morality, character, etc. are of equal or greater importance than his or her ability to pass examinations. But on the other, we feel uncertain about whether we really want the responsibility – and the power – which go with the job, in the way that parents have it. Sometimes we hide behind the idea that we ought not to try to replace parents: but nobody wants to argue for that (though for many children, something as strong as that is sometimes necessary – and not just for orphans). We suffer perhaps simply from a failure of nerve: who are we (we guiltily ask ourselves) to take on such a task? But somebody has to – unless we want to hand children over directly to the street gangs or whatever potent groups they join for lack of any such group in school. Teachers are, admittedly, an oppressed class: beset by local authorities, demanding parents, governors, the law, and battered by (constantly changing) educational fashions and theories. But we should ask ourselves the question 'If these were truly our children (as if we were like parents), how would we organize our schools so as to do justice to them *as people*?' Unless we ask as radical a question as that, pastoral care will be no more than just another educational fashion, generating its literature, its bureaucratic structures, its in-service courses and all the other paper-apparatus so regrettably common in education.

Chapter 11

Selection and grouping

If we are going to have schools or other educational institutions we inevitably face problems about how pupils are to be allocated to them and how they are to be allocated to different groups within them. These problems are often discussed under headings like 'integration', 'segregation', 'comprehensive education', 'mixed-ability teaching', 'setting', 'streaming', 'banding' and so on, but they are best described as problems of selection. Can anything both general and helpful be said about what criteria we should use?

I think it can, but we want first to remind the reader of those particular benefits or goods in which we are interested as educators: namely, benefits directly derived from *learning*. The criteria of selection that are appropriate to these benefits are not necessarily the same as those appropriate to other benefits. To take an example from another sphere: if we were selecting a team of chess players for a top-grade international competition, we should naturally want to select the best chess players. But it might be that some other people would be offended if the team did not include some members who were from ethnic minorities, or Catholic, or women. Thus there would, or might, be a conflict between criteria of selection derived simply from good chess playing and criteria derived from the importance of politics, or diplomacy, or whatever we would want to call it. How we settled such conflicts would depend on the comparative importance of the goods in either category. But we need to be clear – as, in this case, it would be extremely clear – both about the difference between the two sorts of goods and about the criteria of selection appropriate to each.

We shall here restrict our concern to educational goods and the educational activities that promote them. There are some strictly logical points to be made. For any activity (A), we may formally say, there will be constituent criteria (C) such that, without C, A is logically impossible. Since activities necessarily involve people doing things, all people engaging in A will need the ability and willingness to satisfy these criteria (call this 'personal ability/attainment and motivation', PAM). Therefore all As require PAM, via C. For instance, let A be 'playing football': then C will consist of the minimal criteria for the playing of football (the keeping of certain rules, in particular), and PAM will consist, for instance, of knowledge of these rules, the desire to abide by them most of the time, and the physical ability to move about, and so on.

This is worth stating formally, if only to drive home the point that we are not here talking about 'keeping up standards' or doing things well, the desire for which may be one inspiration of educational ideologies sometimes labelled 'traditionalist' or 'élitist'. We are concerned not with these or any other ideologies but with something much more fundamental: we are talking about what is logically required for things to be done at all. Thus a group of pupils who could not or would not play musical instruments pretty well, follow scores, etc. could not do anything seriously to be described as 'playing Beethoven'; pupils who did not know much Latin and Greek could not be described as 'appreciating classical literature'; and so on. It is not that their skills could not be described as mediocre; rather, it would make no sense to give these descriptions to what they were doing – just as we should not call it 'playing chess' if someone quite ignorant of the moves and pieces pushed chessmen around the board.

These simple points are worth remembering because it seems abundantly clear that whom we select ('segregate' or 'integrate'), when, and for what purpose, will depend on what activities we want to go on. If we want As that require PAMs that are possible for only a very few (Olympic pole-vaulting, for instance), then no argument is needed: the PAMs will be very hard to achieve, but they are logically required for the As. Similarly, if the A is less demanding, as perhaps in 'learning to read', 'learning about numbers', 'learning about the environment' and so on (compare 'reading Sophocles', 'doing differential calculus' and 'taken pollen counts'), the nature of the PAM follows from the definition of the A. So it seems that the most sensible way to go about this business is first to determine what As we want to go on in education and then see what PAMs these require; and this exercise in itself should settle many issues about selection by reference to straightforward logic. Once we have decided that we want a particular educational activity, A, to go on, the learning groups select themselves: anyone with the relevant PAM can (and, if we think the A to be universally valuable, should) engage in the relevant A; conversely, no one without it *can* engage in that A. Criteria of other kinds (social class, wealth, colour, parental inclination, etc.) are simply not relevant at all. Thus if we think that an A described as 'appreciating literature' is educationally valuable for all, and the PAM for this is 'being able to read to standard S', then anyone with this PAM can and should do A, and no one else can. It may be said that, for instance, the irrelevant criterion of wealth (perhaps being rich enough to live in a 'desirable' neighbourhood with a 'good' school) does, in fact, segregate pupils in a way that prevents the operation of the proper criterion: that is, pupils who do in fact have the relevant PAMs are not able to engage in the relevant As. But this is simply to point out that we are using the wrong criteria, no doubt because of some kind of social injustice that hinders 'equality of opportunity' – that is, the giving of all pupils *with appropriate* PAMs the chance to do A.

It is not accidental that in educational practice we recognize the obvious force of the logic above most easily in areas that have a clear and definite structure. In many schools it is the mathematicians above all who are in favour of 'setting', 'streaming', etc. partly at least because it is quite clear that mathematics involves stages of learning, and that pupils must have gone through one stage successfully before they even begin to tackle another (we have to learn to add before we can multiply, and so forth). But all subjects have some conceptual structure of this kind (think of the concepts with which a pupil must be familiar and the understanding he has to possess in order to make sense of an Act of Parliament, Newton's Laws, the trade winds, a sonnet); and there is an enormous job to be done, in each subject, by way of mapping out these structures. Mathematics is not a unique case. This is the danger (whatever may be the advantages) of using very general titles like 'the humanities', 'environmental studies', 'language' and so on. The titles do not, even indirectly, specify just what is supposed to be learned by particular children in particular times. As soon as we get down to specifying this, the particular pieces of learning can easily be seen to be structured and subject to the sort of criteria we are talking about. The danger is that we may never bother to specify in this way.

If we do not even attempt this job, various As that may be important might easily perish by default. For example, suppose an A is described as 'English' in the timetable, such that it has a fairly clear structure, involving fairly specific and perhaps fairly high PAMs at different stages (the ability to learn grammar, correct spelling and punctuation, the desire to understand non-contemporary literature, etc). Now, suppose we react against this because the PAMs are too high, we think, for the average pupil: we then replace this A by another A (still called 'English') with quite different criteria, more easily satisfied by more pupils (the ability to enjoy some magazine articles, 'creative writing', etc.). In this situation the original A may *simply disappear*: it is not that we are teaching the same thing, 'English', by new methods – we have redefined 'English' to fit what we take to be the average pupil's PAM. The same move may be made with almost any subject-title.

Instead of starting with a list of educationally desirable As, trying to get the pupils' PAMs to fit as required and honestly abandoning (for some children anyway) these As where we cannot get the required PAMs, there is a temptation to take some level of PAM (perhaps that of the 'average pupil') as given and then to tailor all our As to fit that level. Thus suppose we have a class of 30 pupils, and we have the option of activities A1, A2 or A3: and suppose that all the pupils can manage A3, whereas only 15 have the requisite PAM for A2, and only 5 for A1. One temptation is to settle for A3, allowing A1 and A2 to go by the board. The opposite temptation involves doggedly persisting with A1, leaving 25 pupils out in the cold. The only way of avoiding both is in some sense to select and overtly to segregate: that is, to arrange for 5 of the pupils to do A1, 10 to do A2 and the remainder to do A3. It is not here relevant whether we do this by putting them in different schools, different 'sets' or 'streams', or different corners of the classroom: the point is that they are segregated simply by virtue of their engaging in a different A.

We want to stress that this leaves certain questions entirely open: in particular, the question of how much value we put on various As. It would be logically possible, if implausible, to maintain that vast numbers of As are not particularly valuable – not only activities that are commonly regarded as 'highbrow' or 'élitist', such as the understanding of Latin and Greek literature, higher mathematics, textual criticism, etc. but also such things as a grasp of scientific method, correct English and computation and an appreciation of good music. These and other examples, if one got down to the business of spelling out the relevant PAMs clearly, would be seen to involve much more specific, and perhaps more demanding, PAMs than we might at first suppose. Those who take their lead from preconceived PAMs might find themselves cutting out more As than they would like. But the move could, of course, be made. Our point here is that the question of whether to make such moves can be settled only by a careful consideration of the As as PAMs we are dealing with – something that rarely happens.

There is one point (we think a strong one) in favour of starting with the As and trying to tailor the PAMs to fit them rather than vice versa – at least as an overall strategy. The point is simply that whereas we can determine the nature (if not the desirability) of As, and hence of the PAMs they entail, just by hard thinking or sheer logic, it is much more difficult to accept PAMs as given or determinate in isolation from any A. First, though it is not, of course, absurd to talk generally about a pupil's 'motivation' or 'interest' in learning, we naturally want to ask 'Motivation for what?' 'Learning what?' As we all know, a pupil's 'motivation' or 'interest' may vary very widely from one subject or activity to another. Secondly, while we cannot do anything practical to alter the logical entailments between various As and PAMs, we can and should do a great deal to alter the PAMs themselves. How much a pupil can 'be motivated' to do or to learn will depend very much on how much 'motivation' we give him or her.

In this respect we have to guard against not only misleading models of human learning that may be encouraged by the term 'motivation' itself, but also certain fashions or prejudices that may unduly limit for us the kinds of incentives or 'motivation' we can in fact bring to bear. One thing that may set such false limits is some kind of theory to the effect that certain motives are bad in themselves, or worse than others, or 'developmentally' inferior in terms of some set of 'stages' leading towards 'autonomy' or 'intrinsic motivation'. It is quite unclear to us that there is any proven, or even any intelligible, theory of this kind; and in this case, one might well be prepared to endure the (hardly intolerable) guilt of using 'inferior' incentives (for instance, fear) in order to produce desirable results (for instance, that pupils should actually learn to read and refrain from bullying or knifing each other). Another quite different point, practical in nature but surely smelling even more of fantasy rather than common sense, is the fact that teachers are simply not empowered to bring certain incentives to bear. This needs to be changed.

In any case, if we did take different pupils' PAMs as given, or to the extent that we did, similar arguments would apply. Because the PAMs are conceptually connected with the As, there will be certain things that people (with a given PAM) logically cannot do and certain things that they can. Suppose we prefer to start from some idea of 'what suits' the pupils rather than from the idea of certain As being somehow intrinsically valuable: then the As that 'suit' different pupils will necessarily be different simply because of the different PAMs. If one person is not 'suited' by, say, higher mathematics – because his or her IQ is too low, or because he or she is bored, or because of whatever we are prepared to take as satisfactory evidence – then another person with a high enough IQ or sufficient enthusiasm or whatever *will* be 'suited' by it. In other words, whether we start with the As or with the PAMs, the conceptual connection between the two drives us to differentiate. People are just, in logic, 'selected' or 'segregated' in this way, whatever practical arrangements one may choose to deal with this; and to turn one's back on this fact altogether implies a refusal to make any educational judgements at all – the claim, in effect, that as we have no idea what As are of any value, or what PAMs pupils have, we might as well lump everything together.

We have seen that any activity demands some selection, but the same point holds good even if we do not wish to engage in *activities* at all. One might imagine a person who dislikes segregation arguing as follows:

> We won't have any 'academic' As, like learning mathematics and Latin and so on, because a lot of pupils are not up to this in any serious way. So we'll have very simple As, like swimming and playing games together. Oh, but wait! A substantial minority, for one reason or another, cannot swim or play games properly. All right, they needn't *do* anything. They can just *be* together – it's a good thing in itself to have working-class children mixing with middle-class children, blacks with whites and so on. That at least isn't subject to 'criteria' that exclude people.

But, of course, it is. We may succeed in mixing working class with middle class or black with white; but now, what about redskin children? Have we got enough fat children in the school? Is there a proper mixture of pretty and ugly pupils? Are we not excluding people from say, the north of England (Irish children, pygmies etc.)? Indeed, is it not exclusive and 'segregationist' to have just children in schools anyway, as we are keeping out adults and keeping in pupils?

Some criteria must apply, because it is logically impossible to use *every* criterion. Even if we say, 'Schools should include everybody', that must mean 'everybody within a certain area'; and even if we go beyond this and import people from abroad, we cannot import them all. Some people, by chance or design, will be left out: and in the extreme case in which nobody is left out, we should not be talking of a particular institution at all – we should be talking of the whole world. Hence we can talk of schools or any other institution not as 'selective' or 'non-selective' in general but only as 'selective' *by reference to some criteria*. This (obvious) point is sometimes missed because in many debates 'selection' is given an over-specific meaning. People are easily bewitched by the specific practices and institutions that are before their eyes; much as 'examination' tends to be interpreted in terms of specific (written or institutionalized) examinations, so that people too readily take up a position for or against 'examinations', without bothering to remember that some form of examination in the wide or non-technical sense would be a necessary feature of any system of sustained or serious learning (for one thing, serious learners would want to be as clear as possible about how much progress they were making).

Can we even talk of schools as *more* or *less* 'selective' except by reference to specific criteria? It may seem that we can: surely school X, which demands, say, that its entrants should both pass an entrance examination and live in the neighbourhood, is more selective than school Y, which simply demands that they live in the neighbourhood. But in practice this distinction is illusory; for we have to assume that the school will fill its places, and then the extent of the 'neighbourhood' will be different. School X will have a wider neighbourhood or catchment area on which to draw, since it will draw only those who pass the examination; school Y will have a narrower neighbourhood, since it is committed to taking all the children within it. The addition of one criterion relaxes the force of the other for school X, and the absence of the (academic) criterion in effect makes the criterion of 'neighbourhood' more stringent for school Y.

There is an important point here, worth noting because it does, we think, partly account for the feelings of many people who claim to be 'against selection'. Some rough distinction can be drawn between 'human-made' and 'natural' criteria of selection, and there are many people who resent the former but tolerate the latter. Thus it may seem to such people that the 'human-made' criterion of passing an entry examination is more objectionable than the 'natural' criterion of living in the area. As this example shows, the distinction is often difficult to sustain in practice: there are human or 'human-made' reasons why people live in certain neighbourhoods (e.g. they can get a job or afford a house there) – people do not just grow naturally in neighbourhoods, like wild flowers. It is, in fact, quite hard to think of criteria that are not, or could not be, affected by human action – features which are totally 'natural'. Even such features as height or physical strength or intelligence can at least be diminished or stunted by human behaviour.

But in any case it is not clear why these 'natural' criteria should be preferred. People do indeed differ in, say, their skin colour or their physical attractiveness, but why should these criteria be preferred, in principle, to such 'human-made' criteria as, say, a person's social position or the passing of a certain examination? It may seem that by merely allowing the natural criteria to operate and by not positively enforcing criteria of our own making, we somehow evade the terrifying responsibility (some might think, the guilt) of 'selecting'. But this is clearly an illusion: failure to act, to enforce our own criteria, is as decisive as acting. Thus, to take a parallel, if we allow cattle to become the property of the strongest or the most cunning, rather than enforcing laws of property, this must mean that we prefer the criteria of strength and cunning to whatever other criteria those laws represent. Generally speaking, indeed, we seem to believe that 'human-made' criteria represent some improvement on 'natural' ones.

What other worries could we have about selection in general? For the trend of our argument so far suggests that the only thing we have to worry about, as educators, is the question of what educational activities (As) we want to go on: we can then, as rational beings, select only those people who can profit by these As – that is, those with the relevant PAM. If we do not, our sincerity in saying that we want those As to go on will be in doubt: just as, if someone said that he wanted a Beethoven symphony played well but did not select members of the orchestra by reference to their talents and willingness as musicians, we should question what he originally said. This is, indeed, in broad terms the correct conclusion; but it is important that we should do justice to any doubts that might remain.

The chief worry is represented by an idea associated with the desirability of 'integration' for the specific educational purpose of what we may call 'moral' or 'social' education. But for this purpose the most natural way in which we should think education relevant, surely, is that educators should have the direct and immediate task of educating their pupils *out of* the domination of irrelevant criteria. We do not, after all, think that people's identity or self-esteem should turn on their social class, or religious affiliation, or wealth, or whatever social criteria may be current in any particular society. We are talking here about the task of moral education or the education of the emotions; and if we take this seriously at all, presumably the chief message we want to get across is that pupils should not put undue stress on social distinctions, that these distinctions do not ultimately matter, that they should not care too much about whether they are working class or middle class, black or white, rich or poor, pretty or ugly. We want them, of course, to acknowledge the facts; if a pupil is bad at mathematics or football, or too fat, or poor, we do not wish to mask these facts or pretend that they are otherwise. On the contrary, it is an essential part of their education that these facts should be faced. Somehow as educators we have both to do this and to give the facts no more than their due weight.

For obvious logical reasons, it is impossible to do this unless (for at least some of the time) we actually attend to these facts and distinctions. For example: in so far as pupils are or may become racially prejudiced, the feelings here have to be brought out into the open and moved in the direction of reason. Little or nothing is gained educationally simply by 'mixing': the pupils have to learn somehow that a proper concept of a person is based not upon race or colour but upon other criteria, that the needs of all persons have to be respected, and so on. If they have inclinations that run counter to this rational procedure, these have to be acknowledged, inspected and somehow changed.

It is, certainly, a significant fact that, for the specific business of moral or social education (as against, say, learning mathematics), the pupils bring their data with them, as it were: that is, pupils in the same school cannot help but learn about each other, the people they actually mix with. But it seems a very open question how relevant this fact is or in what direction it points. If one wished them, for instance, to grasp and apply some notion of 'kindness to animals', what 'mix' of animals would be educationally the most desirable? Would we feel guilty about *only* having hamsters and cats and rabbits, 'segregating' (by accident or design) cows, elephants and aardvarks? Should we feel guilty about only having such-and-such a range of pupils, within which there will certainly be plenty of variation in terms of age, personality, appearance, taste and so on, and set about 'integrating' morons, aristocrats and (if we can find any) Martians? If so, our guilt is logically endless.

This does not mean that it makes no difference what 'mix' we have. For example, we might wonder whether the pupils would really grasp the concept of 'kindness to animals' if they only had one kind of animal – say, hamsters: might they not grasp only 'kindness to hamsters'? So too, if they only had one kind of fellow-pupil: for lack of experience and interaction, they might not find it easy to grasp the concept of a person if the only people they ever saw were, say, clean-faced Catholic girls of an obedient disposition. But all this is uncertain and turns very much on what we ought (for this purpose) to count as 'one kind of'. It is too easy merely to assume that the criteria of differentiation we are worried about (e.g. colour, creed, class) are the ones that form the chief impediments to pupils' moral development, and that we best overcome these impediments by having a 'mix' that does not use these criteria. A lot of empirical research needs to be done, but I am inclined to think that educational success here turns on quite other factors, mostly to do with methods of moral education that are more general in character.

A second worry is that the application of certain criteria of selection makes substantial numbers of pupils feel like 'failures', destroys their self-confidence or prevents it from developing, typecasts them as failures (an image that they then live up to), gives them misguidedly low expectations, etc. Since learning any activity, as we have seen, necessarily involves some acknowledgement (however disguised) that certain people have higher attainments than others – some know X already, others have not reached the stage at which they can even start learning it and so on – the argument must presumably point to some much more general sense of failure, perhaps springing from, or (more likely) symbolized by, 'academic' failure in schools, but going far beyond that. Merely the realistic recognition of one's own abilities and attainments, whether in learning or in other things, cannot be wrong; and if this (obviously desirable and anyway inevitable) recognition develops into a general sense of failure, the clear implication is that schools are failing to educate their pupils in other ways.

We must, again, remember that since some kind of selection (by the application of some criteria) is logically inevitable, the argument must presumably be taken to refer to the specific criteria currently under fire: e.g. in the UK different types of secondary school, 'setting', 'streaming' and so on – that is, selection by ability, or attainments, or (correlating to some extent with these) social class. The argument must therefore make the assumption that pupils' or adults' 'self-image', 'self-confidence' or 'sense of being valued' is primarily dictated by their social position. The line is that whether I value myself will turn, first and foremost, on such things as whether I pass some examination, or am in the 'A' stream, or am a member of a particular social class, or make a lot of money. Some of these (the last, perhaps) are more plausible than others; none, to my mind, is very plausible, and certainly none is proven. Sociologists will, of course, stress social factors; that is their trade, and such factors are easier to point to. But we are here talking about psychological states of mind; and psychologists would point, much more plausibly, to such factors as loving parents, good pupil–teacher relations, adequate personal relationships and so forth. One might reasonably suppose that the amount of 'self-confidence' or 'sense of failure' in people is reasonably constant or at least depends on basic psychological factors, and that particular social systems and distinctions simply give it a certain form – in the UK I worry about not being upper-class, in the USA about not making enough money, in ancient Sparta about not being brave or strong enough, in monasteries about not being holy enough, and so forth.

We do not, of course, deny that in some sense individuals' valuations of themselves are 'dictated by their social position'. If the term 'social' is stretched far enough, to include (for instance) a person's infantile relation-ship with his or her mother, or the question of whether there is a kind teacher to take an interest in that person, then it would make no sense to deny it: 'social' is now being used to cover any source of influence except the genetic. But in a more normal sense, which related roughly to the general structure of the larger society rather than to the smaller groups of which the person is more immediately a member, the proposition is at least highly dubious. Do we, in fact, believe that any reasonably sophisticated notion of 'valuing oneself' could be due to 'social' factors in this sense? It is not, after all, until many formative years have passed that the child is seriously aware of such factors.

It should strike one here that our uncertainty about this is, once more, due to our regarding the problem as a social rather than an educational one. If we were really concerned with 'a sense of failure', 'self-confidence' and so on, we should have a clearer idea about how these could be generated and, in consequence, a clearer idea about the sorts of groupings (in schools, houses or tutor groups, or elsewhere) that would be suitable. Thus one might advance the idea of grouping pupils according to psychological type, on the analogy of mental hospitals: we might have one group for the over-confident or bumptious or arrogant, another for the depressed and downcast. Or perhaps, thinking now of successful achievement, we should want to keep those of similar PAMs (see page 102) together, since those of very low PAM would find it hard to succeed at anything in the face of competition from the more able and competent. It might, indeed, turn out that how they were grouped made little or no difference, but rather that everything depended on certain kinds of personal relationships and attitudes on the part of the staff.

These first two worries have close connections with a third, couched in terms of prejudice, intergroup hostility or 'divisiveness'. One of the more curious assumptions here seems to be that the more you 'integrate' or 'mix' people, the more distinctions are abolished, and this too seems psychologically naïve. There are two possible weaknesses here. First, the distinctions may simply change: for instance, we mix social classes only to find that 'socially divisive' groups arise based on different criteria (as for instance, style of dress or taste in music); and these groups may be hierarchical, so that general self-confidence is not improved. Second, the initial distinctions may simply be reinforced: if, say, a tenderly nurtured set of upper-class pupils mixes with a more toughly nurtured set of working-class pupils, it is not at all clear that the result will be to produce mutual understanding and admiration – the effect may simply be to reinforce or even to generate prejudices and stereotypes, to drive each group in on itself and to produce greater defensiveness and even paranoia. (It is not obviously true, to use other examples, that the more men mix with women, the more they like them; or that the more international sport is played, the more international understanding is advanced.) Clearly, much – I think almost everything – will depend on the way or context in which the 'integration' or 'mixing' is done. Perhaps it would be more efficient simply to accept the groups that pupils *themselves* make (which would certainly involve criteria such as common interests and lifestyles, no doubt connected with social class) and work on those: we might get further by accepting differences between groups and classes and making special educational arrangements to ensure that pupils of one group mixed with those of another whenever we thought educationally desirable – perhaps not very often, but often enough (if, indeed, frequency of contact is relevant) to ensure that they recognized and respected each other for what they were.

Naturally, this is a matter of empirical research, but no competent research is likely to be conducted unless we agree about what counts as success. We have somehow to get away from the fantasy that the mere existence of different groups, 'selection', 'barriers' and so on is somehow bad or disreputable. There is, we suspect, a feeling that even if we all succeeded in educating our pupils to feel self-confident and to respect the worth of other human beings, we should somehow have failed if they then chose, as adults, to live in separate social groups, pursuing their own interests and not mixing much with those whose interests were different. Behind this is not only the idea that 'Walls divide and must come down' (compare 'Good fences make good neighbours') but also a deep feeling of isolation and insecurity; as if, by breaking down barriers and sweeping everything together, we could somehow achieve more conviviality, or fraternity, or love. But love, like every other human enterprise, depends as much on the maintenance of rules, criteria and some degree of segregation as upon 'breaking down barriers'. We have to pick the right criteria.

Chapter 12

Competition

If you can meet with triumph and disaster
And treat those two impostors just the same ...

(from Kipling's If)

There are two reasons why Kipling's sentiments are unfashionable. The more obvious one is that we disapprove of his ideology: it seems (to some of us) arrogant, brutal, sometimes racist or fascist, certainly élitist, lacking in concern for the underdog, insufficiently tender-minded. Less obvious is our dislike of his style and descriptive terminology, which is apt to repel us because it is dramatic, full-blooded, lurid and eloquent. This second reason is more insidious, because it may prevent us from facing logical and psychological facts which merit descriptions of this sort. I shall argue that this is particularly true in the case of competition.

Kipling's thesis in the two lines above might be explicated or formalized as follows: Triumph and disaster, success and failure, winning and losing, are inalienable features of any human life; we ought to confront or meet these features squarely, rather than denying or trying to mask them. We ought not to be taken in by them (they are impostors), but rather to recognize that neither of them are ultimately of the highest importance. These propositions would contrast with a policy (for education or social life) which maintained (1) that we could get rid of, or anyway greatly diminish, these features; (2) that they should in any case not be stressed but rather masked or played down, because (3) they are very important, since they inevitably mark people for life (making people feel either arrogantly superior or humiliated failures).

It is perhaps already plain that much educational theory and practice favours the second line of thought. This is generated by the worthy (but, I claim, short-sighted) desire to save children from mortification or humiliation, to increase their self-confidence, to avoid odious comparisons and to promote co-operation between people rather than open or veiled hostility, measuring of one's self against another, and uncaring self-aggrandizement which the term 'competition' suggests. Few teachers or parents who care seriously for their own or other people's children are unmoved by such thoughts: the desire to save whom one loves from pain – or, more moralistically, from arrogance – is part of love. So we yearn, consciously or unconsciously, for a school or a society in which individuals are not subjected to the pain of being judged, graded, failed, punished, made to feel small.

For the child (and hence ultimately for the adult) the psychological roots of competitiveness lie somewhere near the possibility or impossibility of competing against his or her parents – in male-dominated societies particularly against the father and all that he stands for. Many societies outside Western Europe have – in their past history if not in their present practice – been institutionalized in such a way as to make such competition impossible. In Freudian terms, the Oedipus complex is not allowed to surface, as it is considered to be too dangerous and disruptive. Children are conditioned by various means to accept (sometimes virtually to worship) ancestors and ancestral standards; to avoid direct confrontation, even in argument, with other individuals and particularly with elders; to preserve their own and other people's dignity by an elaborate set of social rituals and conventions. Of course aggression and competition are apt to break out in forms all the more violent for being disallowed and unmediated (one might say, unpractised) in education or family life: it is not accidental that many atrocities over the last 50 years have come from societies in which children were heavily indoctrinated with the duty to obey their parents. What is lacking here is the idea of accepting and *working through* the child's aggression: not allowing it to flourish unchecked, but not denying its existence or the need to give it some context in which the child can face it, deal with it, remain psychologically in touch with it and at the same time control it. Most of what we call 'competition' can be seen as offering such contexts.

I am pointing here to the immensely strong temptation to deny certain passions or at least to deny their force. All young children inevitably have passionate desires, and almost any attempt to fulfil them brings them into some kind of conflict or confrontation with others. There will be rivalry, jealousy, humiliation, hubris, despair, joy: that is, triumph and disaster. As we grow older we come to terms, to some extent, with all this: though that too often means that we deny (because of the pain) rather than adjust. It survives in instances where denial is difficult: to lose the person one loves to a rival in competition is, of course, disastrous: to gain him or her, triumph. So too, perhaps, with the honours and rewards which the world has to offer. To accept one's passions and wants as legitimate, as requiring fulfilment, is to accept competition. Not to compete can be a sign of despair: people who are above the battle may be frightened of losing.

These are logical, not just contingent, facts: they derive from inevitable conditions of childhood (smallness) that surround any creature that is to win consciousness and control from a mass of blazing and unmediated desire, in a real world which takes no account of egocentric wishes. The parent's and educator's job is, precisely, to mediate between the two. But there are also some more obvious – though often neglected – and, as it were, pedestrian, logical or conceptual points that need to be made about competition in particular:

1. Competition in a broad sense is inevitable for anyone who wants to perform *well* at anything, since the notion of performing well is relative to other performers, all of whom are out to satisfy certain standards. To be a *good* athlete, novelist, French-speaker, etc. means to perform well in comparison with other athletes, etc. I cannot help but measure myself against them – not necessarily with a vindictive or egocentric desire to do them down, but certainly with some recognition of how well each of us satisfies the standards of the activity. Success and failure, judgement, assessment of merit and the whole constellation of concepts that the notion of standards carries with it are inevitable, whether or not they are marked in any formal way.

2. Some activities, among which are activities which we value highly, are by their nature or constitution competitive: for instance, chess and other war-games, formal debates, tennis, Olympic athletics and so forth. We could, of course, simply dismantle or abolish these, but one would have to be thoroughly convinced of the wickedness of competition before doing so.

3. Most important of all, there is the point that there is no necessary correlation between the *form* and the *spirit* of various activities. A formally competitive game like tennis may be seen, by the players as well as spectators, as a work of art mutually generated by competitors who are primarily concerned to produce a good game, and concerned with winning only as a means to producing it: conversely a formally non-competitive activity may be conducted in a spirit of unnecessary and unpleasant emulation ('I bet I've helped more old people than you have!' one pupil was heard to say). It is an open question whether formally competitive activities (a) encourage the emulation, envy, arrogance etc. which we are frightened of, or (b) diminish them by giving them comparatively harmless outlets.

We touch here on the crucial point that the unpleasant features which are (too naïvely, I argue) associated with the external form of competition derive from elements in human psychology which go much deeper than external forms. Arrogance, lack of self-confidence, envy, the desire to do other people down – all these are inherent in human life. I am not at all saying that we must accept them: rather that curing or diminishing them is a long and difficult task, not to be achieved by simple strokes of the administrative pen which change only externals and do not touch the underlying spirit. I have more to say about this later.

If we accept the psychological background and the logical truths mentioned above, we shall naturally place great importance on ritualized or institutionalized methods of channelling and educating the forces which emerge in competition. Here we need to beware of a largely unnoticed (though everywhere obvious) ideology which tacitly assumes that the only respectable relationship between human beings is one of equality. That is, of course, perfectly true at a certain level: there is no good reason for preferring the interests of one person to those of another (other things being equal) – for instance, for preferring those of husbands as against wives, either in bed or out of it. But, as this (I hope not too indelicate) example may show, it would be absurd to conclude from this that *every* context of human interaction must take the form of a side-by-side, egalitarian seminar. There are times when one gives, and the other takes, orders and commands: when one dominates and the other is dominated. This may be done by allocating spheres of influence (the woman may be boss in the kitchen), or by simply taking turns: and it would be a very frightened, insecure sort of person who needs to regard such arrangements as somehow second-rate or dangerous. We do not have to speak in dramatic terms ('sadism' or 'masochism') to face the facts that all human beings need – sometimes – to dominate and be dominated. A great many activities (sex is only one example) would be watered down beyond recognition if that fact were not faced, and if the need were not given a ritualized or institutionalized form. Indeed much of the egalitarian security and self-confidence we seek is achieved precisely by going through such rituals: by becoming aware that we can show aggression – even have full-scale rows – without ultimately losing our personal security, that we can survive intact without denying our passions.

It is even important to be able, not just to accept or swallow, but positively to enjoy these passions. To use an autobiographical example, I well remember how an article I wrote on indoctrination was immediately followed, in the same book, by an article by another philosopher, proving beyond reasonable doubt that I had got it wrong. He did this in the nicest possible way; but of course, at the time, I felt embarrassed, ashamed and a bit angry (for I had more to say). Later I came not only to realize the ultimate irrelevance of triumph and disaster when doing philosophy (since only the truth really matters), but actually to appreciate and enjoy the way in which this demolition job was carried out: just as it is possible to enjoy being thoroughly crushed on the chessboard by an expert. It is of the utmost importance to confront one's personal dignity by these pieces of reality: the dignity receives a temporary wound, but flourishes all the more for being able to face and overcome it.

In this light the fashionable idea of 'competing against one's self' seems to me a cop-out: a well-intentioned one, since the idea is to protect the dignity of pupils by not branding them failures by comparison with their peers, but a cop-out just the same. Apart from a slight air of unreality about the suggestion (pupils are not daft, and usually know quite well who does what better than whom), the crucial psychological point is that each of us has to face, and accept, the merits and demerits of our performance as measured against those of others. Certainly it is important to be able to internalize the idea of competition and of achieving standards: that is, to measure one's self against the standards inherent in the activity, without the constant need to stimulate one's self by having competitors around the place – just as externally imposed discipline should, to some extent and at some stage of development, be replaced by self-discipline. But it is an open psychological question to what extent and at what stage this should happen. It is also not at all clear that an internalized conscience, which may make one feel a failure because one never succeeds in living up to one's own standards, is less tyrannical than the external pressures of other competitors: that too is an open question.

In so far as these points lead to practical educational conclusions, they might encourage the idea that, so far from trying to protect pupils against competition by simply masking or avoiding it, better protection may be given by a programme which would immerse them in it and thereby persuade them to take it in a more light-hearted manner. That, of course, accounts for the popularity of games and other ritual or institutionalized forms, which are clearly not just the result of imposition by competition-mad educators but natural to human life. The wise educator will ensure that the competition is not conducted in too serious or earnest a manner, but in the way that games properly played are supposed to be conducted – with sportsmanship, enthusiasm but not fanaticism, and with the clear message (spoken or unspoken) that the winners are not thereby proved better people nor the losers worse.

It will be said, perhaps, that none of these points goes very far in remedying the arrogance and sense of failure that distresses us in many pupils (and, come to that, adults). I think in fact that a willingness to face, rather than mask, experiences of triumph and disaster does go quite a long way in this direction; but if we want to go farther we must take a much more radical line than that currently adopted. The way into this can be seen if we assume a situation in which we want to give confidence not only to pupils who are good at work or games, but to others. So then we may go for multiple criteria of success: we reward pupils who are good at music or woodwork, or collecting milk bottles, or practically anything. But this well-intentioned idea runs up against the awful truth that some – actually many – people are not very good at *anything*, a truth which only the romantic deny. They cannot primarily be valued as *performers*, and if we try to do that we succeed only in making them more aware of their inability. Hence the multiple criteria idea, though useful up to a point, is inadequate: we need rather to challenge the whole notion that confidence ought to rest upon performance.

Naturally to some extent the notion is sound: every human being is a performer, an agent, in the public world, and some of a person's self-confidence or feeling of failure will inevitably be connected with that. But at a deeper level the notion is clearly ridiculous. Parents do not love their children, nor do the children feel loved, because they *perform* well (though that may play some part): as Iris Murdoch puts it, love has nothing to do with *merit*. The parents love their children because they are theirs, for their own sakes: and this emerges not primarily in performance – which should rather be viewed as a spin-off from a confidence acquired otherwise – but in such things as hugging and cuddling the child, sharing food and other things, talking with and listening to him or her, giving unconditional affection together with a reasonable amount of structure and discipline, and all the things which any psychologist (indeed any sensible parent) advocates.

I do not deny – rather I want to stress – the difficulty of treating triumph and disaster as (ultimately) impostors in a society, indeed a world, which is highly competitive and gives substantial rewards to winners while robbing losers of every kind of advantage (including, sometimes, their lives). We may hope, certainly, for a society (country, world) in which such things are more governed by justice and less by uncontrolled aggression. But meanwhile we have to prepare our pupils for society as it is, and as to some extent it will always be. Here again the reaction of educationalists is apt to be ideological. Either we wish, along the lines mentioned earlier, to deny the facts and over-protect our pupils so that they cannot cope with competition at all; or else (and some right-wing politicians certainly talk as if they believe this) we take competition to be some sort of end in itself, as if we believe in the survival of the fittest as a moral principle, and regard the goods of this world only in the light of prizes rather than as satisfactions of human needs. Much educational and political debate between left and right is backed, more or less consciously, by naïve monistic ideological positions of this sort.

In opposition to both of these, we should presumably say to our pupils something like this:

There are two truths you should grasp:

1. Perhaps regrettably but certainly inevitably, it will always be neces-
    sary to compete. We have to defend our territory, earn a living, fend
    off our enemies, survive in a hard world. Some form of internal
    competition amongst ourselves may sharpen our abilities to do
    these necessary things. So you must learn to spend some time in
    doing these things.

On the other hand:

2. Only a lunatic would suppose that winning a war, or coming top in
    some economic competition, or achieving high social status, are
    ends in themselves or constitute a very significant part of the
    meaning of life. Competition is a means, not an end; you can enjoy

it, but not take it too seriously. The triumphs of winning and disasters of losing are important, but not of ultimate value.

The most interesting – because the most difficult – case is the case of war. Again, an over-protectionist will deny that there can be just wars (opposing Hitler, for instance), while a Fascist (in the literal sense) will maintain that war is in some way a natural and desirable state for man. So what message do we transmit to our pupils? What attitude does the rational man adopt when engaged in war? Following the two truths mentioned above, presumably we say something like:

1. Sometimes, regrettably, competition in the extreme form of war is necessary to preserve one's self and other people against injustice and misery. You must learn and equip yourself to engage in this when necessary, if only as a last resort. You must learn to tolerate it, to fight hard in a just cause, and (since fighting well may involve this) even to enjoy some aspects of it and engage whole-heartedly in it.

But,

2. you must always remember, in a central part of yourself, that the whole thing is (to say the least) regrettable, wasteful, horrific. You must always have one eye on the benefits of peace and the purposes for which, unfortunately, you are fighting. You may enjoy triumphs and lament disasters, but not with the *whole* of yourself: however important it may be to win, you must remember that winning is not what life is about.

It is perhaps clear from this example how such lessons can only be learned by someone who is, first, able to confront and accept his or her own passion and aggression, and use them in the actual business of fighting, but also able to rise above them or to stand aside from them, so that he or she does not become totally immersed in them. Only such a person can avoid being swallowed up by one or other of the two deceptive ideologies I have described. In recent history, it is not too hard to detect a movement from the uninhibited and expansionist imperialism which we associate with Kipling and the British Victorian Age, to the much more tender-minded, quasi-pacifist and essentially anti-competitive ethos of the welfare state and egalitarian educational ideology: together, perhaps, with a swing back of the pendulum towards a more tough-minded and *laissez-faire* concept of human life which some associate with recent governments in Britain and the USA. Psychic splits of this kind can only be cured by attention to the relevant concepts, and by some deeper understanding of the passions involved.

Part IV

Social and political issues

Chapter 13

Equality

In many societies today it is virtually impossible to read any document about educational aims or goals without bumping up against such phrases and terms as 'equality', 'equal opportunity', 'equal access', 'equality of outcome', 'equal rights' and so forth; and there is of course an immense amount of literature on the topic. The underlying assumption seems to be that 'equality', or some phrase of the form 'equality of . . .', is at any rate an intelligible and sensible educational idea, but that we may have different views about what sort of equality should be pursued. The assumption seems to me wrong; and I want here not so much to add to the literature as to undercut it.

If, as I shall try to show, the assumption is false, this will be because we have not paid close enough attention to the words we use, and have been somehow bewitched into thinking that they have a certain kind of sense when in fact they do not. That this should happen on so large a scale ought to be no surprise to philosophers. Indeed there is one very obvious point which should have alerted us to such a possibility: the linguistic fact that it is entirely natural for someone to say 'It's not fair', or 'Justice, O King!', but odd to say 'It's not equal', or 'Equality, O King!'. That does not mean that there are no connections between justice and equality; but it does at least arouse the suspicion that equality has been, as it were, wrenched away from its natural use and has taken on an unnatural life of its own.

In what follows I shall be concerned only with equality as an *educational* ideal; and we ought to reflect (more fully than I can here) that equality may make sense in some contexts and no sense in others. Equal shares, equal voting powers, equal rights for women, equal division of the spoils – all this is sensible: but nothing coherent could be meant by, say, 'equal conversations', 'equal personal relationships', 'equal religions' or 'equal learning'. It looks as if some human activities simply do not lend themselves to the context of distributive justice at all. If that is so we should expect (what in fact we shall find here) that in our concern to remedy injustice we have taken some activities to be essentially distributive when in fact they are not. Indeed this distinction figures importantly in the upbringing of young children: they have to learn to distinguish contexts in which they can reasonably demand equality, fair shares, and distributive justice from contexts in which these notions are inapplicable: between, for instance, the distribution of sweets on the one hand and personal relationships with the opposite sex on the other.

I

Does 'equality' make sense as an ideal? The ambiguity of 'make sense' (roughly, between (a) 'is a sensible/reasonable idea', and (b) 'is logically coherent') leads me to consider the notion of equality of opportunity first; philosophers are, or should be, primarily concerned with logical coherence, and only secondarily with what is sensible or reasonable – something which goes well beyond philosophical limits, though philosophers may still have something useful to say about it. Moreover (a severely practical point), quite a lot of people with some kind of egalitarian learnings have found 'equality', in some interpretations of that notion, too ferocious or too obscure an idea to entertain as a practical ideal in education and other fields, and have consequently retreated to what seems to be the more accommodating ideal of 'equality of opportunity'. The movement of thought is, roughly, something like: 'On consideration, we do not want everyone to be equal or the same, and it would be misguided to try to make them the same; but at least we can give them equal opportunities or chances.'

It also seems to get round a familiar difficulty: familiar, at least, to those who have taken the point made earlier, that many of the goods in life cannot be simply distributed or rationed, like cake. (On this see for instance Hare, 1977.) This is because these goods have to be acquired or taken up or produced by individuals, so that there is no way in which they can simply be *given* them. Thus (a) *some* kinds of 'resources' (money, time, etc.) can be allocated equally, and (b) *some* 'outcomes' or rewards of education (degrees, salaries in after-life, etc.) can be allocated: but (c) learning, the actual process of becoming educated, is something individuals have to *do*, and what they do depends to a great extent on themselves. But (it is argued) we can at least allocate *opportunities* for learning.

However, this turns out to be controversial. The point is an interesting one not only in itself, but in demonstrating the importance of J.L. Austin's carefulness in distinguishing such things as opportunities, entitlements, powers, rights and so on (Austin, 1961). Consider the game of Monopoly. All the players, we may say, start level or equal. All (we may also be inclined to say; but see below) have the same right or entitlement to build hotels on their property and collect the rent for them. On the other hand, not all have the power/faculty/ability to do so. At the beginning, no one has, since they have not yet collected property cards or amassed enough money; and even later, some players will have greater skill or faculties than others. What about equal opportunity? Is it sense to say that they all have an equal opportunity to build hotels, when in fact some are (for whatever reason) unable to do so, or less able than others? Perhaps it is not.

To see this, consider cases where a person is quite unable to do X. Given a particular situation on the football field, a player on one team may seem to have the opportunity to break through the opposing players and score, but is quite unable to do this: the player is too fat or too weak. Or someone leaves the door of the cell open when the prisoner is asleep: does the prisoner have the opportunity to escape? Does he or she have a chance of escaping? Surely we should say not. The prisoner has the opportunity only if he or she has the power. We could say, perhaps, 'There was a chance ...' or 'The opportunity was there, but ...'; and these phrases make use of some idea of what some other person – an ordinary (awake) prisoner, or a normally competent football player – might be expected to be able to do. I have in fact no opportunity to fly, lacking wings. The point is a subtle one: 'opportunity' and 'chance', it seems, may actually in themselves *refer* only to certain sets of space-time conditions, but we *use* 'has the opportunity to ...' only when she also has the power. 'Every American boy can be President' does not mean 'Every American boy has the opportunity to be President'; one only has the opportunity or chance to be President under a quite severe set of conditions. What it means is that no American boy is legally debarred from attaining the Presidency.

'Well, but we are talking of the opportunity to be educated: and that is something anyone can do.' But we now remind ourselves that 'being educated' is not only not a true passive – that we are really talking of *people learning* – but also comprises a whole host of different kinds of learning. The idea that everyone is equally good at learning, that their powers are equal, is clearly false (consider autistic children or morons): so that, although anyone recognizably human can do *some* learning, or learn some things, there will be many other things which not everyone has the power or ability to learn. I cannot learn to appreciate certain paintings because I am colour-blind. Of course we can envisage an ideal world in which everyone's basic abilities, motivation, attainments and other endowments are sufficient to learn everything (if 'learn everything' makes any sense, which it does not); but in such a world it might be difficult to distinguish one person from another, and in any case it is not our world.

There is the further point, worth making because it applies also to rights and entitlements, that a good deal of learning is sequential in the simple and non-controversial sense that one has to have learned A in order to learn B later. In Monopoly one has the right, or is entitled, to build hotels *if* and *when* one has collected appropriate property and can pay for them, i.e. at some later stage of the game: just as one only has the opportunity to do so at that stage. In education, these rules of the game are replaced by the rules of logic: I am not entitled to learn what check-mate is before I have learned what check is, not because some social rule or disbarment prevents me, but because it is not a coherent thing to be entitled to do.

It seems that the best we can salvage from the idea of equality of opportunity is that there should be no social rules or other factors preventing or inhibiting me from learning whatever I want to or can learn: that it should not depend, for instance, on my social class or wealth or colour or sex or anything of that kind. If I (a) logically can learn X, and (b) have the power or ability to learn X, then I should be entitled to. That looks harmless enough (and of course the inhibiting factors mentioned above are indeed disreputable, because – if other things are equal – irrelevant). But it still will not do, because of scarcity of resources. There will always be such scarcity, because the number of aids to learning is infinite: we must think not only of schools or universities or books, but also of conversations with the best teachers (or parents), educational trips abroad, ease of access to libraries, time for reflection, and so forth. Resources are inevitably scarce, and some of them not in principle able to be equally distributed (for instance, parental love during infancy). So we are reduced, unwillingly perhaps, to the idea that at least we can distribute as many resources as we can equally, even if we cannot coherently talk of equality of opportunity. We can now talk perhaps of equality of access, or resources, or something of that kind.

II

But is even this (to go back to our original distinction) (a) a sensible/ reasonable idea, or (b) a logically coherent one? It is fairly easy to argue against (a). Suppose we consider some resource or access-possibility, such as having a computer to use, or a university to go to. Then we shall say, surely, that (since resources are scarce) we want to hand out computers or access to universities to those who can make the best use of them. And this will apply to all *educational* resources, since such resources have to be made use of if they are to be educational. Because individuals vary in their ability or willingness to *take up* the resources, we locate them wherever there is the best uptake. As an ageing philosopher, I can of course be given an Olympic-style pole-vault along with everyone else, but it seems pretty pointless if I have no ability to use it; and if there are not enough pole-vaults to go round, I cannot complain if I do not get one.

It may now be said that we can at least distribute equally in those cases where everyone can use the resources; for instance, everyone can profit from some form of higher education, so that the resources we have for higher education can be equally allocated. But that still will not do, since (a) not everyone can in fact make *as good* use of higher education as everyone else, and (b) there will be some forms of higher education which cannot be distributed equally without vitiating their nature. Briefly, it is our normal practice to *start with* some educational activities and contexts which we think important – for instance, playing in an orchestra, or learning about relativity theory, or Olympic pole-vaulting – and *then* allocate resources for these by the criterion of who can best profit from them. We can only get round this, and save the notion of equality of access or resources, at the cost of dismantling all such activities: that is, all activities which (by their very nature) are selective, and demand certain standards of attainment and motivation from those who are to partake in them.

Something like this has, perhaps, actually happened in many contemporary educational institutions. We first insist that everybody (or, an important difference, everyone in a particular catchment area) attends the same institution, is taught together (in mixed-ability classes or whatever), and is given the same resources and access: and then we cast around to find learning activities which all can profit from more or less equally. That of course involves dismantling or marginalizing those activities which even extreme egalitarians cannot deny are available only to selected groups, since to establish and resource such activities would be 'divisive' or 'élitist'. That looks like (but is not: see below) at least a coherent policy: but it is, pretty clearly, a policy based primarily on some political or moral ideology, not a policy based on the encouragement of certain specific educational activities. For if we start with valuing certain activities, we shall certainly find that some people are not up to engaging in them (I cannot play in an orchestra since I cannot play an instrument), and hence not suitable candidates for being given the resources to engage. Moreover, there will clearly be some learning activities which are absolutely necessary for fairly obvious political or economic purposes, and which are nevertheless selective in the above sense: we need doctors, research scientists and many others who have to have learned things (and be resourced for that learning) which most of us simply cannot or will not learn. So as a general or universal policy, it seems not sensible or reasonable.

But is it even coherent? This question matters, because if it is we can still pursue it whilst (grudgingly) making allowance for other criteria besides equality: whereas if it is not, we shall have to abandon it altogether. Following a hint above, I want to argue that the notion of an *educational* resource (and this includes access, opportunities and anything else we may *prima facie* seem able to distribute equally) still contains the concept of uptake. For instance, having a computer is only an *educational* resource if it is seen and used for learning: that is, if the owner can actually (and will actually) become more educated by his possession of it. Without that proviso, it is no more an educational resource than a plaything, or a piece of metal, or a status symbol. Of course we may now retreat to saying that we should distribute *potential* educational resources equally: for instance, that everyone should be able to buy the same amount of books, or have the same access to public libraries. But in view of the fact that many 'potential educational resources' are very hard to distribute at all (think again of parental affection), this amounts to saying no more than that *irrelevant* barriers to learning should be abolished: that being poor, or black, or whatever, should not be offered as a reason for debarring people from learning. Of course that is true: but we have first to have a coherent notion of *what* we are debarring or not debarring people *from*, which takes us back to what is surely the correct policy of first establishing the learning activities which we think important, and then ensuring that all individuals who meet the criteria of selection for those activities are not debarred from pursuing them.

It is unsurprising that talk of equality and equality of opportunity (access, resources or anything else) flourishes at a time when many people are strangely reluctant to come clean about just what educational activities they do think to be important and worth establishing: that is, when some sort of relativistic position is adopted towards the merits or demerits of any and every such activity. Naturally if we do not think there is anything, or anything clear, to say on behalf of or against this or that activity, then we shall take our cue entirely from some egalitarian notion of what all pupils can in fact do or learn, not from any notion of what is worth doing or learning. I doubt whether anyone really holds such a position when it is presented to them clearly, since anyone who teaches or in any way encourages learning is obliged (logically obliged) to select some activities rather than others, presumably by some criteria or set of reasons rather than by tossing a coin or throwing dice. But then those criteria and reasons, as I have tried to show above, force us to recognize the incoherence of equality as any sort of educational ideal.

Chapter 14

Diversity I: multicultural education and special needs

I   MULTICULTURAL EDUCATION

'Multicultural education' is now a familiar term; but we need to get behind that title, and behind the practices which now go on under that heading. First, in what way is a person's culture (race, colour, ancestry, etc.) *important*? In determining whether something is 'important', a reasonable candidate for singling out in accordance with a particular criterion, educators are commonly (and rightly) influenced by social or political facts. These facts vary, sometimes dramatically. Any serious educator would want his or her pupils, if they were living in a racist society, to appreciate certain facts which pupils in other circumstances would not need to appreciate. Pupils come from certain backgrounds into school, and will have to live in certain backgrounds when they leave school. We need not teach them to endorse or agree with all or even much of what happens in society; but if they are to survive we have to teach them what the prevailing features and norms of society actually are. None of that (I imagine) is seriously in dispute.

Nor is it in dispute that governments, representing particular societies, have an obligation (putting it at its lowest) to avoid certain kinds of trouble. We do not want civil war, race riots, the oppression of particular groups, or various kinds of crime. More positively, there are certain basic goods (of a fairly down-to-earth utilitarian kind) which we want established: health, a decent standard of living, and so on. In order to avoid the troubles and achieve the goods pupils will have to learn certain things, and the educators will have to teach them those things.

However, few educators believe (at least on reflection) that their task is wholly exhausted by the demands of government or society. They believe – and this belief is encapsulated by the term 'educate', when contrasted with such terms as 'socialize' or 'indoctrinate' – that their pupils should learn certain things which are good or important or worthwhile in themselves, or for their pupils as people in their own right, not just for their pupils as members of a particular society at a particular time. We do not (I hope) teach our pupils about music or literature or religion or morality just because this will be useful to them as social functionaries. These and other types of learning, or other aspects of the learning, are not justified by social values; they are justified by other kinds of values.

Like any other educational question, a question like 'How important is it that these pupils are black (Jewish, Asian, female, etc.)?' has to be answered in (at least) two different ways. (1) We have to consider what we may call the *contingent* importance of these criteria, which would clearly vary considerably depending on whether the pupils were in Alabama, South Africa, Iran or North Oxford. (2) But we would also have to consider how important the criteria were *sub specie aeternitatis*, so to speak, or in the eyes of God; whether (to use less grand language) we want the pupil to think that, irrespective of what their particular neighbours or societies may think, it is a matter of great importance *to themselves* that they are black (Jewish, etc.). There is a *general* question about how much weight or value a person should (for instance) attach to his ancestry, or racial origins, or culture, or class, or creed, which is not exhausted by – not really even touched by – the question of how much importance these features may have in the eyes of others. Whether to 'be Jewish' (whatever, indeed, that means), or how Jewish to be, and what to do about it if one is brought up as a Jew, are all matters which are relevant to a person's life in a general way: not only relevant if one is being persecuted.

If we tackle the aims of multicultural education head on – and it is best, as I have tried to show, not to do this too quickly – we shall find it difficult to rise above the level of the obvious or merely banal. Thus it is obvious (a) that we shall encourage pupils to reflect upon, and (we hope) accept the reasonableness of, certain propositions about the equal value (worth, rights, importance) of human beings as such, irrespective of race (creed, sex, colour, etc.). Moral philosophers have expended a lot of ink on this topic (see particularly Hare, 1981), and I need not enlarge on it here. We may also reasonably want (b) members of one race (culture etc.) to learn something about members of other races: perhaps as an objective in its own right (a kind of anthropological education) or perhaps as a reinforcement to (a). These aims are fairly non-controversial. Much more difficult are the questions (c) how far ought an individual to find his or her identity (sense of security, etc.) as a member of a particular race? and (d) what is to be said about the merits and demerits of particular ethnic cultures?

I stress that these questions arise in the minds of pupils, however much educators may try to side-step them. A girl brought up in a strict Islamic family, or a boy brought up in a Jewish family, is bound to ask how far she or he wants or ought to follow the particular precepts and behaviour patterns laid down by these environments. Such conflicts occur more obviously in a multicultural or pluralist society, but (particularly with increased communication in a shrinking world) the possibility of conflict is always there. Unless educators do something to steer pupils through such conflicts, they are not likely to do more than utter platitudes about human equality (a), or offer a shop-window tour of various races and cultures, without giving the pupils any reasons for preferring one to another (b).

Questions (c) and (d) are clearly linked, at least in that the merits and demerits of particular cultures may have *some* bearing on whether or not to identify oneself as a member of this or that culture. People who like to think of themselves as English (Aryan, African, etc.) do not attach themselves to the *word* 'English'; they characteristically think there is something about English culture, traditions, history, etc. which is meritorious, or anyway which they have some *reason* for adhering to and identifying with. The pretence, often indulged in by multi-ethnic educators, that 'one culture is as good as another' is no more than relativist rhetoric: no one seriously believes that, for instance, a belief in Aryan supermen, or female circumcision, or other such cultural items is just a matter of taste or morally neutral. We think that the question of their rightness or wrongness is a real question.

So far I have done no more than point to some issues which (in my limited experience) are commonly evaded. Even this may be of some practical value: if they were put on the multicultural agenda, and actually *discussed with the pupils* (rather than played down for fear of giving offence), much would be gained. However, there is a good deal more to be said about these questions; and it may help to say some of it here, however tentatively.

I have used terms like 'race', 'ethnic', 'culture', etc. somewhat indiscriminately; but anyone seriously facing the question of what to put their psychological money on (so to speak) would demand much more precision. Even 'race' alone is obscure: are we to say that white people in England are a single race, or a blend of different races (Celts, Angles, Saxons, Normans, etc.)? Different from this is the notion of colour or physical appearance: different again, though commonly confused, is some supposed similarity in terms of geographical area ('Caribbean' or 'Indian' may be used like this). 'Culture' is worse still: I have seen no definition of this term with any serious pretension to clarity.

This matters, because we should be inclined to make very different judgements about 'importance' depending on just what we were supposed to be judging. Thus *prima facie*, and in the light of pure reason rather than prevailing social facts (which we have, at this stage of the argument, put on one side), there seems nothing particularly important about being black in itself: one has to find very specific contexts, such as casting *Othello* or distributing sun-tan lotion, even to see any relevance in having a black skin. 'Because X is black', in other words, is a reason with very limited application. At the other end of the scale, 'being a Christian' or 'being a good all-American democratic guy' ('English gentleman', etc.) seems much more important, since the values and behaviour enshrined in these phrases can at least be plausibly represented as good reasons for a great many contexts in life.

Two temptations meet us at this point, both of which have to be resisted. One is to take the view that education should give no weight at all to individual attachments and put all the weight on impersonal criteria of relevance and merit. If for instance we are concerned with selecting and training a football team, then our practice should be guided solely by the criteria relevant to football: whether particular individuals are psychologically attached to other criteria – whether they are to see themselves as black, Christian, all-American, etc. – is simply not to the point. Relevant considerations in educational grouping and other practice would, on this view, be derived only from what was to be learned: the standard inherent in the particular subject. If we teach mathematics or musical appreciation, then it is simply irrelevant that some mathematicians are Jewish, or that particular kinds of music have particular psychological or social connotations for various people. ('They're playing our tune, darling' is of interest to someone involved in a personal relationship, irrelevant to someone judging the aesthetic merit of the tune.)

The attraction of this view is that it leaves the educator free to disregard (again, except in so far as he has to serve contingent social or other interests) *all* the criteria we have been talking about. The educator can say, in effect, something like:

> Look, we live in a prejudicial society, about which you need to know some facts (some people are barmy and hate blacks/Christians): we will spend a bit of time preparing you for the society you'll have to face later. But apart from this, *just forget* whether you're black/Jewish/Asian/Christian, and concentrate on learning various things in their own right – mathematics, not 'black mathematics'; literature, not 'feminist literature'; religion, not specifically the Christian religion. We shall try to get you to see and love what is *good*, not what happens to be the possession of any particular social or other group – not even if it is *your* group. Of course, as sensible educators, we shall take full account of (as the Americans say) 'where you're coming from': we are not so stupid as to think that your cultural (national, racial, etc.) background makes no difference to how we teach you. But it makes no difference to our educational aims.

Unfortunately there is a snag with this. Briefly, 'Because it's mine' does seem to be a satisfactory reason for certain kinds of attachment, even if I recognize that what I am attached to lacks public merit. In Shakespeare's *As You Like It* Touchstone describes his wife Audrey as 'a poor thing, but mine own'; even granted the correctness of his judgement, we still think it right that he should love her as his wife. I am attached to my home, country, children, even my cat, not because I think them better than others but because they are mine. 'Breathes there the man, with soul so dead, / Who never to himself hath said, / This is my own, my native land?' Well, many may so breathe; but we pity them. Love has nothing to do with merit.

Children, as Aristotle says, are seen as extensions of their parents: a friend, as he also says, is *allos autos*, another self. It is difficult to see how such local attachments could be wholly absent from any form of human life; and even if they could, human life would be much the poorer.

This throws us into the arms of the second temptation, which is (briefly) to adopt a wholly relativist position. We are to take 'important' simply as 'important to X' (where X is some individual or social group). That would demolish both the problem of what categories or criteria of demarcation to use (because each person could choose his or her own criterion and be beyond the reach of criticism), and the problem of what to judge good or bad within each category. Thus we should, on this view, have no objection either to a person finding his or her identity primarily in terms of his ancestry or colour, nor to him or her thinking that (for instance) white was good and black bad.

There are more objections to this than can be mentioned here – not least the point that no one in fact really adopts the position: it would remove the whole idea of acting for a reason, something which is just as firmly written into any form of human life as the idea of local attachment. Here it needs only to be pointed out that the concept of education itself involves the notion of truth or reason, via the concept of learning. To learn something is not merely to change one's mind or behaviour: it is to change them in the direction of truth. If we abandon this idea, we have as educators no reason for doing anything: for choosing one book to put in the school library rather than another, for saying certain things about the physical world rather than certain other things, still less for expending large sums of money on schools. If no change has the backing of reason, there is no need to learn anything. Certainly there is no point in taking the education of racial or cultural groups seriously: for to take anything seriously implies that there are things that stand in need of improvement, and if the criteria of improvement are purely relative we have no ultimate reason for backing one set of practices against another.

We are thus obliged in education, as indeed we are in life as a whole, somehow to put together or do justice to both local attachments – 'Because it's mine' – and public criteria of merit – 'Because it's good'. Some palliation of our difficulties may be found in the fact that some attachments are non-negotiable. We cannot, for instance, escape from our own bodies, or our own parents: and one educational aim must be to help pupils to achieve at least good working relationships (to put it rather absurdly), if not a loving attitude, towards these. But the palliation is a small one. It is an open question, much canvassed in the history of philosophical and religious thought, just how attached one should be to one's body, or indeed one's parents. *A fortiori* attachments to a particular nation, race, or culture are profoundly in question. Hence it seems better to accept two different, though ultimately connected, types of educational aim. Roughly, we want the pupils (a) to be able to love and feel loved, to have the capacity to form local attachments rather than being nomadic, unable to see anything or anyone as 'theirs', with that peculiar sense of 'belonging' which is at the heart of love; but also (b) to be able to make proper judgements about the merits not only of colour or culture or race but of other things that may be more or less worthwhile or trivial.

I must again belabour the point that we must not, as educators, foreclose these matters by making overt or concealed assumptions about the general *form* of a person's identity. In much education today, indeed in much of life generally, it is taken for granted that 'social' identity and position are all-important, and that 'society' (whatever that term may mean: I have seen no satisfactory account) must somehow come into all education. (At a university where I once taught this became a joke in the course titles: 'Mathematics and Society', 'Beethoven and Society', 'Greek grammar and Society' . . .) 'Society' has, it might be said, come to occupy a place previously occupied by other candidates – God, nature, the soul, truth, reason, beauty. How far pupils ought to define themselves socially, how much money they should put on social as against other features of their lives, must be put to them as open questions. Matters of race and culture are just one instance of a general problem here. Of course we are not educating potential hermits; but neither, I hope, are we educating people who see themselves only, or even primarily, as members of this or that society or group – particularly since not a few such groups seem, to put it mildly, somewhat less than satisfactory.

It follows from this that education aiming at (a) and (b) above – the ability to form attachments, and the ability to make judgements of merit – cannot be based on any particular social, racial, cultural or other kind of grouping: for to do that would be, precisely, to foreclose these issues by predetermining the criteria for the pupils. Certainly we may use such groupings as subject matter for discussion, just as we may consider other possible groupings (a club of stamp collectors, a football team, membership of a school); but that is a very different matter. A first step here would be to make an adequate set of categories of attachment, which could be used as something to put before pupils for discussion and experience. We could then have some hope of answering the question: 'What kinds of attachments are there, and what value can we reasonably place on each?'

It will be said, of course, that schools *as they are* (an important qualification) are comparatively impotent, and are forced to accept prevailing social criteria, so that the question is not in fact open – the pupils arrive with particular ready-made identities. That is not entirely true; but even if it were, it would be a powerful argument for greatly increasing the potency of schools as institutions. For unless an educational institution is capable of providing a background strong enough to override the pupils' external emotional investments, it can hardly hope to educate in this area at all. Relativistic temptations make us hesitate here, because we find it hard to conceive of a potent school apart from a particular and questionable ideology. But a moment's thought is enough to show us that the values inherent in education itself demand *both* extremely potent institutions *and* institutions devoted to developing reason rather than ideological commitment. A good family is an obvious example (not all good families share a common ideology, in any serious sense of 'ideology': they are potent because they are fraternally binding and their members love each other).

Schools as they could be (and could be without the need for greater financial support or total reorganization) would have something of the potency – not necessarily the partisan values – of the family, of certain schools in the independent sector, or of other institutions that have refused to sell out to 'society' and are unwilling to lie down under social pressure. Such institutions exist, and we can describe their crucial features – a strong house system or 'pastoral' base which overrides the classroom, a full-time investment on the part of pupils, a deliberate shielding or separation of the institution from external practices and values. These notions, once traditional, are not currently fashionable: the obsession with 'society', together with relativistic temptations, have produced a strong if miasmic desire to 'integrate', 'break down barriers' and 'be open'. That, I am arguing, is logically inconsistent with any serious educational aims: education which simply reflects or plays along with 'society' is not education. The educator *withdraws* (to a greater or lesser extent) his or her pupils from the world, and asks these pupils to reflect upon it and upon themselves, to pursue knowledge and to develop powers of ratiocination which will enable them to see the world differently and more clearly. That task has to be done *in the teeth of* external pressures, whether of ideological intervention or the values of the marketplace.

Such an institution is, in any case, required for the aims in (a) and (b). For only there can pupils (a) form the personal attachments and loyalties which will enable them to develop their ability to love (to form other attachments), just as only a genuinely potent and fraternal family can do this: and (b) gain the knowledge and powers of judgement which will enable them to free themselves from those social or other criteria which they may not wish to accept. This is true of any serious form of moral, personal, social, political or emotional education: unless the institution gives pupils a firm and secure base of personal relationships and institutional loyalty, they will not have the moral strength to make any real changes in their hearts and minds. Something can, of course, be done in the classroom discussion and by other forms of overt education; but these will merely scratch the surface unless they appear as a natural extension of a proper educational background – that is, of an institution whose values and practices are potently and obviously devoted to learning rather than social reinforcement.

Granted that some attachments are non-negotiable, and granted also that we can love where there is no merit, there is still considerable latitude for choosing what we shall be attached to. What criteria are we to use? What makes an attachment desirable or undesirable? It is difficult to divorce such questions from even vaster questions about the meaning of life, or what we should count as of ultimate importance. Nevertheless, some separation (if not total divorce) is possible. Thus Richard Peters (1966) in a well-known book argues for attachment to 'curricular activities' (science, history, mathematics, etc.) on the grounds that the goods they offer are (a) varied and less boring than those on offer elsewhere, (b) non-perishable, and (c) non-competitive: and those are, at least, significant arguments, whether or not we agree with the conclusion.

There are three criteria which seem to have some merit in the light of what we should actually say about particular cases:

1. The object of attachment should be something of central importance to human life, or at least not too peripheral. We incline to look with favour on attachments to one's spouse, children, parents, friends, home and native land because it is hard to see how these could be anything other than central to any normal person. Human beings have to some extent a given nature, and what is central is also given; we cannot just *choose* that something be central. Hence if someone has immensely strong attachments to, say, stamp-collecting, or having red hair or eating off solid silver plates, we feel suspicious and may use terms like 'fanatical' or 'obsessive'. We suspect, perhaps, that the person's natural affections have been blocked or (in a literal sense) perverted. Of course we should make such judgements with caution, but we recognize, for instance, the difference between a miser's attachment to money and the attachment of a normally prudent person.

2. The attachment should be to something which is, as it were, rich and not empty or boring. There is, as we say, 'more in' some things than others; and this again is not a matter of choice. There is more in the relationship of a successful marriage than there is in a one-night stand. There is more in people than there is in dogs, more in Shakespeare than in most other writers, more in advanced mathematics than in the mere recitation of one's multiplication tables.

3. The attachment should be to something *outside the self*. Of course we need to love ourselves, but people capable of love will direct it outwards as well. They will find, respect and value things *in the world* – not just in their own body or mind – that exist in their own right. That might indeed help us to distinguish the ability to love and relate from some kind of autism. Here the reason 'Because it's mine' is harmless, since it enshrines the feeling of belonging to, or with, something that exists in its own right, independently of my will or desire. We find happiness by contemplating and caring for things that are real, not by dreaming or concocting fantasies.

Clearly a good deal more needs to be said about such criteria; but if we accept anything at all on these lines, it is hard to see how either race or culture could be very plausible candidates for educators to emphasize. To make race plausible, one would have (like the Nazis) to build up the idea of race to include all sorts of other goods (the 'Aryan ideal'); this is false to fact, and anyway cheats because it is really the other goods that are worthy of admiration. Race is (a) peripheral, (b) empty, and (as normally used) (c) autistic. Culture is *prima facie* more plausible, because some cultures at least – not all – may contain much that actually fits the three criteria: the culture of the Italian Renaissance, for instance. But that is, again, a long way away from valuing one's own culture just because it is one's own; and we have, and should give our pupils, the chance to opt for cultures other than their own which may contain more that is of merit. In any case, the culture of the *school* (as I hinted above) must presumably be based, not upon reflections or microcosms of particular social groups, but upon whatever norms, values and practices are best for education: that is what we must, as educators, insist on initiating our pupils into, so that we cannot accept their own particular cultures as having any priority (though of course we shall not want to trample on them).

II   SPECIAL NEEDS

Much the same problems are faced when we consider another fashionable title, 'special needs'. Here we run up against the problem, obvious in itself but rarely considered, of what is to *count as* a 'special need' or as a 'disability'. In practice what counts as a handicap depends on the norms of the social group that uses the term and, in particular, on the activities or qualities which that group regards as normal or desirable. Most people do not question the prevailing criteria of success within their own milieu; they accept rather uncritically certain standards and prevailing social values. To find out exactly what these values are in our own society demands careful research, but a useful starting-point might be to question the following assumptions about values:

1. *Physical* ability is the criterion commonly used in relation to disability, since physical disadvantages are more obvious than others. More importantly, our society has no real belief in the greater value of the qualities of mind and spirit. A crippled body we understand; a crippled mind we understand in part; a crippled soul barely figures in our utilitarian terminology.
2. *Social* roles and competence will be valued – again, these are relatively obvious. We are concerned with whether or not children can live a 'normal life' (determined in terms of social expectations), whether they are employable, whether they can 'mix well', whether they can take part in the activities current in our society.
3. Predictably *performance* or achievement is highly esteemed in our utilitarian culture. This may be self-evident, but we need to remember that states such as enjoying, contemplating, appreciating, loving or simply being content could also be used as criteria for being 'normal'. We think more naturally of academic success, careers and some kind of productive existence. Intellectual competence is our first criterion for

the more able child; we may stretch this to performance in music and the arts but we do not stretch it much further. Ability to make friends, to care for others or to show patience towards others might be paid lip-service; but no more than that.

The use of any criteria can be challenged. But there are social defence mechanisms that might predispose us to dismiss such challenges to the values mentioned above. We can argue that it is much more difficult to identify advantages and disadvantages if we think of the mind, the heart and the soul than if we think only of the body, or if we try to rely on criteria which might be acceptable across cultures rather than those criteria of success which prevail in our own parochial society. We may point to the practical importance of achievement and of social competence, whatever our higher ideals may be. We may suggest that, to the child at least, such goals as physical achievement and having a job will – whatever our own values – count for more than anything else.

There is some truth in all these responses, but we should not blindly accept prevailing criteria or shirk the task of establishing the importance of some criteria as against others. We have to attempt to justify their importance on rational grounds, rather than accepting the particular values current in our own society or social group. Unless we attempt to do this we simply reinforce social values acceptable at a particular time and impose them on the handicapped (who are the least capable of defending themselves from the consequences of such an imposition). We then need to ask whether or not culture-free criteria of 'normality' can be established on a rational basis rather than on what is acceptable in a particular society.

Our aim, that we set out to *educate* all these children, could be regarded as giving us some rational criteria at least. By contrast, if we lived in a primitive society we might be concerned with hunting animals in the forest, and we might wish to single out the strong and swift as hunters and/or those who were likely to perish in the hunt unless given special support. But today we have the time, money and – apparently – the inclination to view children in a less obviously utilitarian light. We are concerned with their learning; not only with whether or not they have sound teeth, sufficient toys, colour television and non-polluted air. We ought to ask, 'Which children are "special" from an *educational* (not from a social, military, medical or economic) point of view?'

All this may seem obvious, but it is a good deal less obvious than what we think the children ought to learn. We do not, unless we think about it, actually believe that the criteria of social competence and achievement are as valid as we claim. In fact we would probably all admit that learning to make friends (very different from merely 'mixing well'), to love people, to enjoy the arts, to like some kind of work for its own sake (very different from accepting social criteria of employability) and similar achievements are much more worth learning than most of what we put on timetables and in the curriculum. Thus our *actual* (and surely rational) beliefs about what is worth learning seem at odds with what we actually teach. We do not really think physical disabilities and social handicaps are of prime importance. The most important handicaps are those which impede a child from learning (to put it briefly) to be a *person*, not from learning physical or social skills or academic or vocational achievements.

It may make little odds whether or not I have only one arm, whether or not I am paid for my work (I can still *work* – the concept of work is not tied to public or paid employment), or whether I can perform well at various academic or practical exercises. Those are not central to my personal, moral and spiritual qualities. Of course we can try to indoctrinate people into thinking that they are central; we can teach people (often by expressing the wrong kind of concern) that a person with only one arm or without a job is of less value than a person with only one friend or without a sense of humour. But that will depend on us and has little to do with being 'handicapped' in more important senses.

Our prejudices are compounded by the remarkable fact that most great educationalists in the past – and many today pay lip-service to this – have insisted that the education of character, personality, morality and the emotions are at least as important as either the 'academic' or the 'practical' side. But in practice most of our schools regard as 'normal' an educational regime in which pupils undergo a series of subject-based sessions throughout the day. This has the predictable result that in so far as we identify pupils as disabled or (sinister word) 'disturbed' in their emotions, character, or mental health, we tend to pick on those pupils who find it hard to tolerate such an educational regime; those, in short, who cannot 'cope with' (another significant phrase) an educational system which we regard as 'normal'.

If we could imagine an educational regime in which the development of character, the handling of emotions and personal interaction were genuinely valued as central, in which plenty of time was devoted to them and in which a serious attempt was made to foster and assess them, then what we should count as 'normal' and 'disabled' would turn out very differently from what we do today. Emotional cripples would become identifiable as physical cripples are now visible; different *kinds* of 'handicaps', 'advantages' and 'needs' would stand out from the ones we now take for granted.

It may be objected that identification of this kind is so much more difficult than the identification of more easily visible deficiencies of today's 'handicapped' children that we cannot be expected to change our attitudes. It may be argued that we can see well enough if pupils are capable of playing games and doing their 'normal' school work, but not if they are, say, unable to make friends or control their aggression or form relationships with the opposite sex. But, as these examples may suggest, our ability to apply such new criteria is quite adequate, provided we have enough opportunities in school life (and take them seriously enough) for these different qualities to become visible. Many teachers can recognize these qualities already but are short of time or energy to apply them as criteria because of curricular demands. The whole set-up may mask our own fears about the difficulties of educating pupils in any other way. These fears are largely groundless.

The general ideas which guide our *treatment* of handicap flow from the socially acceptable criteria mentioned earlier. An illustration of how prevailing social (and questionable) values dominate what we do is the idea of integration. That it is good to 'integrate' is commonly accepted today. In a hierarchical society with established values and a highly visible class or status system, differences between one man and another are seen as inherently justified. When such a society comes under attack, or its individuals become disillusioned with its supposed justifications, *any* difference becomes tarred with the brush of unjustifiable privilege. There is a fear that, if A is distinguished from B by some criterion or other, the difference will be used to set up another hierarchy in which some are labelled as 'inferior' or 'failures' and others as the opposite; hence the only safe way seems to be to play down or mask or psychologically deny the differences. This is one of the main roots of egalitarianism; any division or separation is seen as threatening. The view that different classes and talents play different parts in a harmonious society – envisaged, for instance, by Plato or Menenius Agrippa's metaphor about the social body in Shakespeare's *Coriolanus* (I.1) – is taken as unsatisfactory, because of the potential conflict between parts. It is as if the only safe form of social justice ought to be based on equality and the rejection of any differences. The stress on 'society' and social competence (rather than on the autonomous and unique individual) contributes to these attitudes.

Plato may have been right, however, in so far as the placing of particular individuals in groups must logically depend on what the group is for. We select players for football teams by the criteria of football, university entrants by intellectual criteria, and so forth. If we are concerned with the education of the children with special needs, the relevant criteria are educational; it is no good putting pupils who cannot add into a group learning advanced mathematics. What must count as a 'disability' or 'advantage' here must depend on the purpose of the enterprise. Educational criteria are often vague and multiple, but they are not indefinitely flexible; when we want to mix or 'integrate' different types of individuals, we are still out to achieve some purpose – and that purpose will determine the type of 'mix'. Physical disability is usually irrelevant to learning Greek but relevant to learning gymnastics; no sense, let alone justification, can be given to any general or overall ideal of 'integration' (or 'segregation').

III   CONCLUSION

The general trend of my argument has been hostile to anything seriously to be called 'multicultural education', and to current practice in identifying 'special needs', because it turns out that there is a mismatch between the concept of education and the use of criteria which have nothing necessarily to do either with learning or with personal security. Educating people has no logical connections with the use of educational institutions for other purposes – to guard, integrate, socialize, indoctrinate or achieve some other political or social end: any more than it has logical connections with the use of these institutions to store arms, for instance, in time of war or food in time of famine. Not everything that goes on in schools is education.

That is not to say that different sorts of people (including different cultures) may not need different kinds of education: of course they do. Very stupid children, deaf children, children with outstanding musical talent, children who will have to spend a lot of time catching seals in Greenland, indeed every and any real or notional group of children brings it own peculiar endowment to school, and leaves school to go into its own particular milieu. That is a conceptual truth; and it follows that they must be handled differently. Nevertheless the aims of education remain constant, and must include the idea of helping pupils stand back, in the light of reason, from all particular backgrounds or commitments, so that they may make up their own minds autonomously on the basis of certain general truths about what is important.

If some government or other agency wishes to use educational institutions for some other purpose, the onus of proof is on it. We should need to be persuaded that, for instance, only bussing black children to white schools would avoid race riots, or that only certain programmes in the schools would keep blood off the streets of Brixton. Politics is politics: if it wants to invade education (or the practice of science, religion, the arts or any other enterprise) it must declare its hand and prove its case. I do not, myself, regard the political case of multiracial or multicultural education (if that education underlines, as it usually does, criteria of race and culture) as anywhere near proven; and the *educational* case seems to me logically incoherent.

We may still ask ourselves, at a very practical level, how we are to handle prejudice and other undesirable things that go on in schools as well as outside them; but the answer to this is not far to seek. We might ask ourselves how these things are avoided, or dealt with, in a loving and well-organized family. The answer is that the structural and other features of the family *override* the possibilities of prejudice or culture clash. The children are profoundly engaged in other activities, they invest in the institution, and (if they were to show absurd prejudice) would be reprimanded or punished, and run the risk of forfeiting the love of the parental figures. In any efficiently run family a great many of the problems which beset schools are solved, as it were, *en passant*. Of course the family is not immune from jealousy, hatred, fear and so forth; but it offers an arena in which these are (a) contained within reasonable bounds, and (b) made subject to education. If we fail to improve the potency of schools, as described above, we shall not be saved by any amount of special educational initiatives under such headings as 'multicultural' or 'special needs'.

To put this less sentimentally: in producing categories like 'multicultural education', 'special needs', 'remedial education', 'life skills' and so forth, we become victims to a kind of terror. Like one who patches a leaky boat, we look round in alarm in case certain groups are not being done social justice to, or certain needs not socially catered for. (This is a never-ending task, since there are an infinite number of groups and an infinite number of needs.) Then we invent special educational programmes to cater for them and salve our consciences. Our feelings here are really (and honourably) political or social: not educational. In doing all this, we lose sight of more important educational categories. 'Multicultural education' for instance, in so far as it means anything clear at all, must presumably be a kind of moral education, and ought to be classified as such: it has something to do with gaining a proper concept of a person, being aware of certain kinds of facts, having the ability to relate to other people (of different backgrounds) in certain ways, etc.; just as 'sex education', in so far as it is not just elementary biology, must presumably be a kind of moral or psychological education, or education of the emotions.

The intrusion of political worries into education thus causes us to lose grip both of certain structural or general features necessary to educational institutions (on the analogy of the family), and of certain basic categories of what it is important to learn (on the analogy of Hirst's forms of thought: see Hirst and Peters, 1970). These two losses are in process of making education even more of a rarity, and educational institutions even more feeble, than they already are. The circle is at present vicious; such feebleness of course encourages governments and other agencies to increase the pressure and hence disable the institutions still further, particularly by displaying a lack of trust. We may be able to reverse this, by thinking hard about the concept of education and what it implies; but I am not sanguine about this, since thinking hard about concepts is not a popular activity.

Chapter 15

Diversity II: gender

Sex and gender are very fashionable, and very high-temperature, issues in education at the present time and the wise teacher will need to think especially hard about them, for fear of being carried away by emotion and prejudice. There is much to think about: all we can do here is to look at what seem to be two of the main problems. The first concerns the notion of doing *justice* to people (in this case, especially to the female sex); the second is about what might be called appropriate political or educational *strategies* for improving the situation in whatever way it needs to be improved.

I   JUSTICE AND SEX DIFFERENCES

Problems about justice in relation to gender in education fall into two categories, which it is important to distinguish. There is the matter of what we may call 'social justice' (1), which applies not only to women but to any other social group (racial, religious, cultural or whatever): we shall be concerned that the members of any such group are not debarred, simply by virtue of membership of that group, from taking up whatever opportunities in education (or society generally) their desire and capacity enables them to take up. Thus 'Because she's a woman (black, working-class, etc.)' is not a good reason in itself for debarring someone from learning science, or becoming a head teacher, or whatever, on irrelevant grounds. We may say that people should have political *rights* or *access* to whatever opportunities they want and are qualified to take up. Here we take their desires for granted, as having political validity: it may be that my nature makes me unfit for, say, being a teacher or studying science or going in for politics, but that is not (at the political level) a reason for preventing me from doing so. But there is also (2) the question of what my nature actually is: whether or not I would be *wise* to take up this or that option; whether it really suits me; whether it fits my actual abilities and motivation. Here we may speak of 'doing justice to' myself and my nature. This is a quite different question, and to be settled by quite different kinds of argument. Not many people think there should be political or legal rules governing who should marry whom or what job one should do, but equally we think it possible to make mistakes about whom we marry or about going in for this or that career.

The particular difficulty with education is that teachers cannot help but advise, encourage (or discourage), and in general make judgements about their pupils, on the basis of their perceptions about the pupils' qualities and what suits them. Human beings are similar in some respects, but different in others. Thus sensible teachers will not (even if they could) positively prevent a tone-deaf pupil from specializing in music, or a colour-blind pupil from specializing in painting, or a less able pupil from seeking university entrance; and they will be aware of the dangers of 'labelling' or 'stereotyping' pupils in such a way that their real capacities are masked or restricted. Nevertheless, teachers have in practice to make judgements on the basis of their differences: and they will also have to have some defensible general view about those differences themselves.

We have here to resist the temptation of two naïve pictures. One is a traditional picture of (in this case) the female sex and the male sex, in terms of which women just *are* such-and-such, just 'naturally' do such-and-such work, and 'their place is' in the home (or wherever): and similarly with men. Such a picture may be backed by some uncritically accepted ideology or religion. Another, now currently much more fashionable, is to deny any significant or non-negotiable differences between women and men: to say that 'really' there are none, or that if there are they can be altered because they are due simply to 'social conditioning' and hence reversible. According to this picture, we should expect equal numbers of men and women in any career or in studying any school subject; and we should look with disfavour on any ('sexist') literature which relies on the view that there are indeed significant differences of personality or psychological make-up.

The fact is that we do not *know*, with anything like certainty, what differences exist between the sexes (or racial or cultural or many other social groups), if any indeed do: nor whether they are non-negotiable; nor whether they are relevant to certain educational choices or arrangements. Yet we have to have some sort of defensible and sophisticated view about this: otherwise we have no basis for judgement about what really suits this or that individual. Of course it is unlikely that absolute generalizations are possible: that *all* women (men) are of such-and-such a kind. There will inevitably be exceptions – perhaps many exceptions. Perhaps no generalizations are possible at all. Nevertheless, we have to consider the matter with open minds. To do justice, like cases must be treated alike: but unlike cases must be treated differently.

It is worth saying in advance that there is nothing wrong with or anything regrettable about people being different: nobody really wants a world in which they are not. To some people, however, differences appear threatening: either because they are just differences, which makes life somewhat harder to handle (though more interesting), or because they are frightened that some differences may be seen as evidence of superiority. It is clearly true that a difference can always be seen in evaluative terms, not because people are lunatic enough to regard a mark of differentiation as showing that a certain group are, *sans phrase*, 'superior' or 'inferior' – though no doubt such people exist, if any sense can be made of what they say – but rather because there is or always could be some context to which a difference was evaluatively significant. Thus, if men are (generally) more muscular, this makes them superior when it comes to shifting rocks; if women are smaller, this makes them superior when it comes to getting out of narrow-mouthed caves. What is important is to establish what differences there are and what they are relevant to.

The major problem about sex differences is the systematic ambiguity of certain kinds of evidence. That there are physical differences between the sexes is not denied. Thereafter, at least at first sight, the game seems entirely open. For if a certain feature F is always preferred, and perhaps *thought* to be 'innate', by a society in the process of child rearing, how in principle can we tell whether F is in fact 'innate' or 'the product of social conditioning'? Thus, suppose that F is something such as 'taking the sexual initiative' or 'holding political power' and suppose further (what is not true) that no societies encourage or even allow women to do these things: how are we to tell (1), whether F is simply not 'in' women and that all societies are vaguely aware of this, so that they reinforce or channel this 'innate' difference or (2), whether there are no innate differences, F being merely 'a social product'? It is, in fact, very difficult to conceive of a way of settling this. For instance, some think that boy and girl babies start to behave differently at a very early age (say, one year) – before 'social conditioning' has a chance to get at them. Does this not prove 'innate' difference? Not a bit of it, other people say; there are differences in the ways that people (themselves 'socially conditioned') handle, cuddle, or look at, or speak to, or in other ways treat boy babies and girl babies, which might account for the differences.

A rather better experiment might consist of either leaving the babies devoid of any human influence from birth – no doubt robots could be designed to feed them, change them, and so on – or ensuring that those humans who did have contact with them did not know whether they were boys or girls. The former sounds somewhat cruel, and the latter a bit difficult, though not impossible. However, a determined environmentalist still might say that the human attendants (in the latter case) made some sort of subconscious decision to treat all, or some, of the babies in accordance with sexual criteria. This would be hard to verify and, although the experiment seems well worth doing, it would not tell us all that much. For many of the alleged differences between the sexes are such that opportunity to display those differences could, logically, only arise after a high degree of human intercourse – and moreover, intercourse that took account of the child's sex. An F such as 'taking the sexual initiative', for instance, could only be verified under conditions that included the subject knowing that he (she) was male (female); and this, it might be said, makes verification impossible, since the knowledge (in a given society) might itself determine F. Social conditioning theories are often unfalsifiable.

There is also another problem of verification, which I mention at this stage to show that there is no easy way out. Some hold that we have only to point to societies (usually in the Polynesian Islands) where women do, in fact, display F in order to prove that F is 'in the nature of' women. But that will only work for *abilities or attainments*. Thus, if a woman can be found to play chess as well as the best male chess players, this would certainly demolish the proposition that no women can reach that standard of attainment; if enough women could be found, we could no longer generalize about women's abilities in this respect. But this tells us nothing about women's *attitude or motivation* in regard to chess-playing. It is mostly items of attitude and motivation that sensible believers in basic sex differences have wanted to rehearse. Thus, if few women hold political power, this may be because they do not want to; in turn, possibly, dependent not upon 'social conditioning' but upon what is 'in their nature'. Conversely, one might come across a society (Amazons) where women hold all or most of such power – but this equally might be due to a certain sort of social pressure, which goes *against* their 'nature'. Nobody denies that social pressure plays a part: the dispute is whether that pressure goes against or along with ('reinforces') some basic feature of their 'nature' – or whether there are any such features to be distinguished from those of men.

It ought to strike us that there is something extremely simple-minded in this sharp distinction between 'innate' and 'social conditioning'. The position seems to be that the physical scientists, the geneticists, and the experts on the brain can point (as yet) to nothing that directly correlates with significant differences. Even if they could, there would be philosophical problems to be solved. (There is something funny, not to be explored here, about saying one inherits a tendency to do *The Times* crossword or run for president in a way that there is nothing funny about inheriting red hair or a tendency to tuberculosis: the difficulty being one of translation from one language, the language of genes and chromosomes and brain circuits, into the language of social action and performance). So it appears to be anybody's guess. Since the evidence of 'social conditioning' is highly visible, this has been seized on with undue force.

There is, however, a whole swathe of evidence of quite a different kind. To associate it with the name of Freud is dangerous, because this might imply agreement with Freud's particular view on women, or with his particular stories (for instance, penis envy); I mention Freud only because he first, or most clearly, drew attention to this sort of evidence and encapsulated it in the remark 'Anatomy is destiny'. It needs first to be shown that there is *room* for this sort of evidence. This can be done, perhaps, by asking whether anyone really believes that the sort of body one has is likely to make *no* difference to one's attitudes, mental postures and general outlook on life, and whether it can fairly be put under the heading of 'social conditioning'. I do not think that anyone seriously believes either, but in case anyone does think so I will give some imaginary examples. Suppose I am born a humpbacked, immobile midget, or suppose I have tentacles, or suppose children were characteristically stronger than their parents – does anyone now think that this would make no difference to psychological attitudes? It would; and the difference would be logically independent of (though always able to be reinforced or diminished by) anything fairly to be called 'social conditioning', even in the widest sense whereby that phrase included parental handling. Equally, it would in an important sense be independent of genetics: certainly it is a physical *fact that* I am immobile, or very strong, or tentacular, or liable to break if something bumps into me, but the fact will cause me to adopt certain attitudes (for instance, fear of destroying things because I am so strong, or fear of being destroyed because I am fragile).

It is important to see that this is a conceptual or necessary point, not an empirical one; for what actual empirical attitudes are likely to be forced on, or at least made very attractive ('natural') to, the actual bearers of bodily differences is a much more difficult and detailed question. We are here in an area of enquiry where one is never quite sure whether to use conceptual or empirical arguments – whether it is a matter for philosophy or psychoanalysis. Most psychoanalysts believe in some story about infancy and early childhood that distinguishes between boys and girls – that is, the story is different for each. The (not purely Freudian) story about the different love objects is a clear example: according to this, boys and girls love their mothers (since their mothers, or stand-ins for mothers, feed them at the breast) but, thereafter, the boys have only to transfer their affections to other (non-incest laden) women, whereas it is characteristic for girls to transfer first to their fathers and then to other men. Even this is, in some aspects, a conceptually necessary story. I mean that, granted that virtually all babies are first fed by and hence in some sense get attached to women, this will necessarily make *some* difference to the subsequent history of their love objects. Much of Freud – almost all that can clearly be shown to be true – consists of conceptual points of this kind: so, too, with other psychoanalysts. *They* rely for verification on a combination of what the patient says on the couch, what the patient's dreams are, what may be observed in very young children, and what his or her involuntary symptoms and voluntary behaviour are in everyday life, apart from the more indirect evidence of anthropology, religion and the like. All this adds up to a perfectly respectable set of verifiable propositions, whatever may be thought of their individual truth and falsehood. But here I shall try to see what can be said on conceptual grounds, combined, perhaps, with a little common sense.

Such conceptual necessities as there are stem from the point made earlier: that young creatures' bodies are bound to affect their mental stance. This is not just because bodies and their interaction with the world are inevitably important to any creature but because the infants' world is one in which their own bodies and, by comparison, other creatures' bodies play a major part – in the absence, that is, of those mental or intellectual features that infants only gradually come to acquire. This is not to say that infants do not have desires and emotions; lacking certain controlling mechanisms, they have them in a more passionate and 'raw' form than adults or even than young children. The point is that the *targets* of those desires and emotions, the material that is likely to shape them and give them direction, will often be something bodily or physical. The difficulty is to determine what this implies for boys and girls.

It seems to imply at least this: that the boy's greater physical strength (in terms of output – I am not talking about endurance) and musculature, together with a certain speed and crispness of bodily movement (boys tend to run faster than girls, throw balls harder, and so forth), are likely to influence his attitude in the direction of *agent* rather than *patient*, initiation rather than response. The possession of a penis, which appears to him to *do* something, as against a vagina, which does not so appear, may reinforce this or be taken merely as symbolic of it. This difference remains with children, other things being equal, until puberty when it is strongly reinforced. Erections of the penis are more obvious and greater physical strength more apparent; conversely, the girl's centre of gravity shifts downward – she becomes more obviously slower and physically weaker by comparison, softer, fatter, and so on: a different kind of object – and certainly a different kind of *erotic* object. There is also, of course, the whole apparatus connected with child-bearing and suckling, which is in itself likely to promote certain attitudes rather than others.

That this will make the two sexes vary in a dimension that it may not be too misleading to describe as 'aggression' seems wholly obvious. Boys come to see themselves more as acting on the world; girls as responding to it. These are both kinds of 'doing' and by no means is the whole of the child's attitude strait-jacketed – boys will respond, and girls will be aggressive. But, in general, we sense the difference that is clear when, for instance, one watches either sex playing tennis. It is not that the girls are, in principle, less well muscled or strong or fleet of foot, yet they hit the ball much less hard and crisply and with less of the 'killer instinct'. It is not at this later age just a matter of physical difference but of engrained attitudes.

Even if this general picture is subject to alteration and adjustment, it may remain true. We must remember that much of the adjustment may itself be due to psychological, rather than 'social' causes. The Freudian story of transferred love objects would be one possible example of such causes; another, just as obvious, would be the effect of identifying with the mother (who, however aggressive, will almost certainly appear to the young child as 'the one that feeds' or 'the one with the soft breasts'). The degree of alteration possible within these (anatomical and psychological) parameters must be limited. It is not absurd to talk of 'the female role' and 'the male role', so long as we are careful not to interpret 'role' too narrowly.

We are talking, not of (other than physical) *ability* (a matter in which, in so far as we can disentangle it from motivation, there seems to be not so much difference between the sexes) but about a general motivational stance.

A word of warning here. It is entirely possible, indeed predictable, that either sex may at some point wish to *deny* or rebel against these roles or stances. (Transvestism is an obvious example: the man is saying, 'I wish I were a girl – if I dress thus I can, temporarily, be one or at least pretend'.) This may happen for all sorts of reasons, most of which are likely to be subconscious. One good candidate is simple *envy* of the opposite sex; men are said to envy women's natural creative powers, and the *couvade* (when men imitate pregnant females) is quoted as a possible piece of evidence; the envy of women for men's roles is also clear. It is, then, by no means necessarily good evidence if a person makes his denial: a man may say 'But I am soft and pliable', or a woman may say 'I am as aggressive as anything, hard as nails', but it is more than possible that they are speaking in an attempt to convince themselves (and others). Contrary to a fantasy that we all like to indulge, individuals are *not*, or certainly not always, in the best position to know what they are really like and what their deepest feelings are: many of them are hidden from us and perhaps more apparent to others (not only our psychiatrist). People create and spend a lot of time and energy in sustaining images of themselves that they need (for some psychological reason or other): images that impinge on the area of sex differences are not immune from this – indeed, the more emotion-laden this area becomes, the more false images of the self are likely to be generated.

How far and in what sort of detail this general account would be verified by psychoanalytic enquiry is a matter beyond my scope: I have aimed here only to show that there must, logically, be *something* in it and to open the reader's mind to the possibility and respectability of that sort of enquiry. Pursuing the account's general implications, however, we can see at least some possibilities. First, it is likely that certain jobs (tasks, services) will, in general, fit or suit one sex rather than the other (again, for motivational reasons rather than for reasons of ability): those that require good observation of people, pliability, tenderness, patience, endurance, and other qualities that might form an expansion of the notion of 'passivity', 'nurturing', or 'responsiveness' will suit women; the more 'active' or 'initiatory' qualities of men fit better into other jobs. This more or less fits the traditional picture; but this is hardly surprising, if that picture is based on some intuitive understanding of sex differences (rather than pure myth). Second, since sex differences will very likely be emphasized in specifically sexual encounters, it is likely that the man will be the wooer or initiator, and the woman, the wooed or responsive. Characteristically, the woman will see herself primarily (I do not say only) as a responsive object and will want to be beautiful; the man is attractive in another mode more connected with activity, strength, and some kind of performance. 'Man proposes, woman disposes': this, too, is traditional though not invariant. Third, it is more likely that the woman will be more concerned with the inner world of feeling, emotion and personal transactions than will the man, who by contrast will 'project' himself more into the outer world of science and abstract thought (it is not, in my view, accidental or 'socially' determined that novel-writing has been one of the fields in which women have excelled – of course, they excel in things which a male-dominated society may not score highly, such as child-rearing or tending the sick). Many women may find the mere possibility of visible achievement vaguely threatening, just as men find passivity threatening or alarming. 'Women keep trying to bring personalities into everything, they never keep their categories clear, they're not interested in *selling the product*', a man said to me once. And a woman, 'Men seem to think that "reasonable" equals "logical": they put things in watertight compartments, they're always trying to *make* something out of the world instead of enjoying it'. Finally, as passive respondents rather than as active initiators, women are more likely than men to want security and men more likely to want variety – this, too, has sexual implications that are traditional.

I think it likely that some, at least, of these differences have a genetic background; it seems unlikely that they are *all* due to the kind of early infantile reaction that I have briefly described. Not that such reaction is insufficiently potent to account for such differences; but the chances are that the physical differences go along with the brain differences, as they clearly go along with glandular and hormonal ones, which also affect the situation. Animal behaviour may be thought to shed some light on this; it is hard to believe, to use old-fashioned language, that Nature did not back the reproductive and sexual roles of the two sexes by some kind of psychological differences having the same general force. The probability is that many millennia of evolution and natural selection, in early human history, have played an important part.

The comparative physical weakness and vulnerability of women is also in itself likely to affect their social position. Such vulnerability – to rape and assault, for instance – will need support and protection from men; and the consequent roles of protected and protector, whereby the woman relinquishes some power of command and initiative to the man in return for her safety, including perhaps the safety of her children, seem virtually inevitable in almost any society. Exactly what that should mean in terms of power and equality is disputable; but here again we seem to be up against something which exists naturally, and not just as the result of social conditioning.

II   STRATEGIES FOR CHANGE

If – a big 'if' – we have as teachers reached some sort of defensible view about what justice would look like in relation to the male and female sex, what strategies should we employ to achieve it? This is not so much a matter of subject-teaching, but of policies and practices adopted by the school as a whole and the individual teachers within it. We may feel that a certain group is not getting a fair deal, and we may want to try to remedy this, even to kick up some kind of fuss about it. What should we do? Answering the question adequately depends on getting a clearer view of what kinds of things we are entitled to kick up a fuss about and what kind of fuss we are entitled to kick up. There appear to be three rough categories here:

1. In some cases I might not have any, or enough, power *as a negotiator* – that is, as someone who ought (as, before any specific deals are done, every person ought) to have an equal voice in deciding on the rules of the game. Disenfranchised women, or slaves, or philosophers might object to not having the vote on these grounds, irrespective of what *other* powers, rights, or treatment they enjoyed or endured. The objection is simply that they have no say in what these powers, rights, or kinds of treatment are to be.
2. In other cases the *treatment* I get under a particular regime may damage my interests: if women are beaten up by husbands, they are, in a clear sense, harmed or damaged. If they have freely contracted for regimes in which this happens, they cannot complain on grounds of justice; but if thcy havc not, the damage highlights, as it were, or gives a concrete demonstration of what harm is done by the imposition of regimes on unwilling people.
3. In other cases, again, I may have some *ideal* (ideology, set of values, particular picture of how things should be) that the regime does not adequately realize. I might think, for instance, that women should be treated more like men, or more like children; that slaves or serfs would be happier if they participated more, or if they participated less, in day-to-day decision-making; or that philosophers should bc sccn as much more, or much less, important to society than they are now seen.

The practical difficulty, of course, is that what we take to be 'unjust' or 'oppressive' regimes usually offend us in all three ways; consequently, we have a naïve idea of 'oppression' and 'liberation' that leads us to view, and react to, what goes on in particular societies in a monolithic sort of style. It is also possible to see why so many revolutionary or liberationist groups tend to base their thinking on some kind of ideology rather than on less esoteric principles of justice. For it will seem to them – often quite rightly – that what *causes* the injustice in cases (1) and (2) is some kind of social ideology – 'capitalism' or 'male chauvinism' – that obliterates both simple negotiating equality and simple justice of treatment. So they are then tempted to *replace* that ideology with another (Marxism, feminism). In just such a way, I suppose, the ideology that led most of the classical Greeks to view women and slaves as in some general way 'inferior' was replaced, or is being replaced, by what one might be tempted to call the North American ideology, which regards everyone as in some general way 'equal'.

Consequently, and understandably, those who want change in such matters are not content to stick with (1) and (2): they also see their task as ideological, propagandizing, or – to use a kinder word – *educational*. It is not enough to free the serfs and thus ensure that they do not suffer from the knout: they must also come to see the wickedness and false consciousness of capitalist society, the truth of Marxist theories of history, and so forth. So with some feminists, it is not enough to have the vote or to receive just treatment in getting jobs, or in trials for rape, or in being paid for housework: they also want men to see women 'in the right way'. This (*per se* laudable) desire is all the more tempting in that there is, in a clear sense, such a thing as 'doing justice to' other people that goes beyond such things – such as seeing them for what they really are, respecting them as persons, or not imposing stereotypes on them.

But the proper vehicle for negotiating *this* kind of business is education and rational discussion. I stress 'education', not indoctrination or propaganda, because many revolutionaries (and of course, many conservatives) make no clear distinction – the distinction between non-pressurizing and pressurizing methods. The fact is, as we know quite well when we stop to think, that we do *not* want to subscribe to a rule in virtue of which we can all impose our ideals and ideologies – our pictures of what it is to 'do justice to' various people and problems – on each other without restraint. This is why we have to distinguish between interfering with people – neo-Nazis, for instance – who are simply propounding their views, however absurd in our opinion, and interfering with people who actually lynch blacks or beat up Pakistanis. It is tempting to blur the distinction, because we feel that words and ideologies lead to deeds; nevertheless, we are right to hold our fire and wait for the deeds, just as we are right not to penalize drunkenness *per se*, but only to penalize it when the drunkard is a manifest danger (when driving, for instance). Without this distinction most of the specific freedoms – including free speech – beloved by liberal societies would rapidly vanish.

Nor is it unimportant to note that there are logical (not only empirical) impossibilities in doing *total* justice, indeed, in doing anything like justice, to other people in this sense. It takes at least a lifetime even to begin to do justice to even one woman. Inevitably – and the point is independent of what particular stereotypes or pictures one has of women – since one does not know all about her, certain features will be stressed, or be 'salient' at the expense of others. Nor should we take 'at the expense of' too seriously – it is to say no more than that one may notice certain things and not certain other things about, say, a Shakespeare play not only on first reading but on any subsequent reading. One notices, perhaps, the plot or certain beautiful lines of verse 'at the expense' of the characterization or certain other lines. Would it even *mean* anything to say that one had done 'complete justice' to the play?

There are two standard reactions here, both (again) understandable but ultimately unsatisfactory. The first is to suggest that, unlike the Shakespeare case, A ought to see B in the way that B *wants* to be seen. (I suppose Shakespeare might be said to have an interest in how we see his plays: but he is dead.) The trouble here is that, if we are now talking about the merits of particular ideals as such (irrespective of who entertains them), there is no particular reason to believe that the way in which B wants to be seen actually represents the right ideal: B, for instance, may be a male-dominated woman in a state of 'false consciousness', and A a truly liberated man (assuming they exist) who sees her as fully equal. Feminist sympathies would then, I imagine, be with A; but then the criterion of how B wants to be seen is useless. We can jump the other way and say that the criterion of how B wants to be seen should be preserved, irrespective of whether B has the right ideal, although now we have jumped back from the promotion of a particular ideology into the area of general equality and justice. This represents the bind in which all overenthusiatic revolutionaries are caught: Marxists have the same difficulty with the working classes who do not (it may seem) actually want the revolution to happen.

The second reaction, somewhat more plausible, is to insist on a much higher standard of at least *trying* to see people 'for what they really are'. Here the Shakespeare case may be preserved, since we might think it morally disreputable, or at least rather slack, not to do our best to 'appreciate' the play for what it was really worth. This brings in the idea of 'using people'. We seem obliged to say that there is nothing positively *wrong* either in seeing people only in certain aspects (as pretty, or good tennis partners, or philosophers) or in restricting the kind of business we do with them to those aspects (kissing, playing tennis, doing philosophy). We might say, at most, that it was rather a *pity* that someone saw *Hamlet* only as a blood-and-thunder thriller; we would, no doubt, encourage people to get as much as they could out of various worthwhile objects and out of each other. But the facts are that there is a limit (again, a logical as well as an empirical limit) to how much time and effort one can put into this.

To put some of this in a more practical way: there are various things that are or might be true about me that, if only by some stretch of a febrile imagination, might be thought to represent various *species boni* or 'standard interests'. Suppose I have a first-class degree from Oxford; or I might be physically appealing, or able to do *The Times* crossword, or good at table tennis. Now, suppose various women keep coming to me and (apparently) wanting to talk about Oxford philosophy or wanting me to help them with the crossword and that few, if any, throw their arms around me and say, 'You handsome erotic brute, you!' If I had too much of this, I should certainly be tempted to say, 'It is all most depressing, they only want me for my brains, really the *stereotypes* women have are awful'; and certainly in any long-sustained relationship, I should hope that they would – and perhaps would actually try to persuade them to – see me as more than a crossword expert or someone who has 'the right sort of degree' or as more than any of the other things that I myself take for granted and that I feel are already more than adequately catered for. Actually, I should probably find that *persuasion* was not a very good weapon: people see one in the way they want to and are likely to extend their range or sophisticate their perceptions of others only by a general increase of trust and experience, not to say love. My attitude basically ought to be, I take it, something like,

> Well, it is nice that they like me for PQR – at least that is something, and we can share that together; and perhaps in time they will come to see that I am also XYZ and that this represents something that can also be shared.

Anything like resentment or coldness or hostility towards them because they did not appreciate all my features, or because they singled out ones that I *myself* did not particularly value, would be clearly unreasonable: the former, because it is logically absurd and the latter, because (among other reasons) what they valued about me might well be more important than what I valued.

It is important that we should want people to be more *educated* (reasonable, understanding, etc.) in this whole area, as opposed to pressurizing them in various ways so as to promote a particular ideal. But how do we do this? Thus, suppose (as I myself believe) that one of the most basic difficulties (perhaps the most basic) is that men and women have certain psychological vested interests that cause them to see the opposite sex in certain ways (even, perhaps, to describe it as 'opposite'). Let us say, for instance, that men are rather frightened of women and uncertain about their mysterious powers, so that, as a kind of defence or screening system, they tend to see them often as conquerable objects, or pretty little things, or whatever. Now, as any competent psychiatrist knows, learning of this kind requires a great deal of trust and security before it can seriously proceed at all: it is entirely useless, and may be worse than useless, to beat individuals about the ears with the intention of making them change their attitude – whatever may appear to happen on the surface, the defences are simply reinforced. When we are incensed about something (even about ignorance), there is a standard temptation to do something that will make people 'sit up and think'. Well, no doubt they sit up, and no doubt they react, and they may even think: but changing an attitude is much more than this. Attitudes have, as it were, a case history that nearly always involves some kind of *fear* – without diminishing this, nothing of much significance happens.

It depends on what we want. If feminists want – what for their *political* objectives may be entirely proper – something like a social tradition in which women are, in some broad sense, accepted as equals, work side by side with men, are allowed to do any job, and so forth, this is one thing. This is rather like saying that we want science, rather than astrology or witchcraft, to flourish in a society: we want it to be, as it were, institutionalized and socially visible. But so to educate people that they come to have a genuine scientific *attitude*, an attitude that they will hang on to despite temptations to the contrary, is something else. Here institutionalization is extremely fragile, as the corruption of science in Nazi Germany and other such cases abundantly show or, indeed, as the modern tendency to go in for astrology and various other non-scientific fantasies shows. There is, then, at least a question about how far – in principle, and ultimately in point of logic – what might be called 'social' or 'administrative', or even 'political', moves can effectively *educate*. They can, of course, help to keep the ring for, or enable preconditions to be established for, education: but, in most important matters, that may be all. People are not educated out of prejudice *simply* by being forced to mix with other classes or colours or creeds: we recognize this because we recognize that there is a conceptual misfit between what is implied by 'prejudice' and what is implied by these 'social' methods.

Many liberationist and revolutionary groups seem to take the view (sometimes even without prior reflection or argument) that most or all educational failure is due to 'society'. Had people not been 'socially conditioned', or if we had a society that removed this misplaced conditioning, it is thought, people would grow up to have just views of the opposite sex, blacks, Oxford dons, and other people in general. This suggests an extremely naïve view of the multiplicity of causes that generate things such as prejudice and misperception: it would be very odd if *some* of the causes did not have more to do with, for instance, the child's early years (irrespective of what sort of parents s/he has) and the unconscious mind, rather than with 'society'. Indeed, there are some necessary truths here, not just empirical facts, on which we have commented earlier. But even if this were not so, only an extreme Rousseauesque or Wordsworthian view of human nature – the uncorrupted, unalienated, naturally good and virtuous child – would enable the founders of a new society to dispense with the task of considering just how its members are to *learn* to see people in the right way.

In considering this, it is tolerably clear that the founders will need more than 'social conditioning'; they will require that the members, as children, come to grasp certain concepts and principles in the light of which they form the appropriate attitudes and behave in appropriate ways. To this, there is bound (even in the ideal society) to be strong resistance, even if only the resistance of one who finds thinking hard and clarity difficult to attain: laziness, perhaps, or original sin, or the egocentrism natural to everyone, or whatever we may want to say – but not just 'social conditioning'. I am tempted to say that, with gender as with any serious problem, anyone who thinks that the right answers are *obvious*, or that it is easy to obtain a just view, or that we can be so *certain* of our views that we can expend our time and energy on furthering a partisan set of beliefs, has hardly even started to take the problems seriously.

Postscript for mentors and tutors

Each institution, and each individual tutor and student, works in its/his/her own way; and any suggestions that are made here are not meant to be followed religiously – or indeed at all, if they conflict too much with the personal styles of the people concerned. Nevertheless, there are some generalizations to be made, and what follows may be of help in the teaching and learning of general professional studies, in relation to this book at least.

I   CONTENT

As I said in the Introduction, no single person or book can hope to cover all the disciplines and types of enquiry relevant to major educational topics. Fortunately, however, there is a certain order of priority in considering each topic, which gives certain disciplines pre-eminence, and (as I see it) justifies concentrating on them in any book which is intended to serve as an introduction. Nearly every educational question (and perhaps every important one) is inextricably involved with *concepts*, *values* and *feelings*. The questions may at some point direct the learner to matters of non-controversial empirical fact – though even here 'the facts' are themselves often disputable and open to different interpretations. There is, I believe, not a great deal of indisputable empirical *knowledge*, whether in the form of 'research findings' or any other form, on which teachers can rely; and in any case the first steps in approaching any topic have chiefly to do with concepts and attitudes. It is this area which we concentrate on in this book: following from discussion in this area, the tutor will be able (with the help of a library and other resources) to direct students' attention to any useful further reading, and also – at least equally important – to relate the points to their actual experience in schools and elsewhere.

In dealing with this area we have two main tools ('techniques', 'disciplines', 'methods', or whatever we may want to call them). Both aim at sophisticating the students' (and tutors'!) common sense, and hence at generating a less prejudiced, more objective, and hence more reasonable set of views. The first is the *analysis of concepts*. We have to ask and answer questions like 'Just what *is* discipline? What does the term *mean*? Is it the same as any form of control? If not, just what is the difference?' Or 'What is "equality" exactly? Do we mean just similarity or homogeneity, or is it a way of talking about justice? What would "equal treatment" mean in education – or in medical treatment?' Briefly and obviously, we have to be thoroughly familiar with the *concepts we use* in discussion and decision-making; otherwise we shall literally not know what we are talking about. The second is *analysis of feelings*. Most of us are heavily influenced by our emotions and basic attitudes towards almost all educational issues – to notions of authority and discipline, to questions about sex and gender, to minority groups, to 'élitist' or 'progressive' educational stances, and so on. Sometimes these feelings taken an overtly ideological or political shape: sometimes they are more concealed, and take the form of fixed prejudices and even fantasies. We have to make these overt, to be able to own up to them, inspect them, and perhaps modify them in discussion and communication with other people.

I want to stress here that using these tools does not mean (1) simply absorbing and being able to regurgitate the results of any very 'academic', 'abstract' and 'scholarly' set of enquiries perhaps entitled 'philosophy of education' or 'psychoanalysis'. On the contrary, we have to make full use of *our own* views, feelings and experiences (especially our experiences in schools and other practical educational situations, e.g., in the family); not merely to receive doctrines from on high that have been worked out by professional or supposedly expert philosophers, or psychologists, or anyone else. For even if these doctrines gave us a complete set of 'right answers' (which is very doubtful), they would be of no use to us unless they connected with our own views and experiences, and hence affected our own attitudes and practice. But equally it does not mean (2) just thinking and saying whatever we like, just swapping points of view. For then we make no progress towards the truth, or towards a more reasonable and sophisticated position. We have indeed to subject ourselves to a kind of *general discipline*, perhaps quite close to that which Socrates deployed on his pupils. This discipline must make us *aware* and *critical* both of the concepts which we use and of the feelings and emotions (often unconscious or semiconscious) which generate our initial opinions. This is *hard intellectual work*, not an opportunity for just 'sounding off' or trying to sell our ideological positions to other people. We have to tolerate doubt, welcome criticism, pursue accuracy in our use of words, admit to our inner feelings, and analyse both the problem and our own responses in a tough-minded way. This can only be effectively done in a context of close communication and trust, about which it may now be appropriate to say a little.

II   CONTEXT AND METHODS

In a way the context of such discussion and interaction is at least as important as the content. As most of us already know, there is an enormous difference between a seminar or discussion which is largely ritualistic, in that people just 'go through the motions' of looking at a problem without having their hearts and minds in it, and one which is somehow more 'real', more demanding, more authentic, and in which we are more fully involved.

There are some obvious moves that can be made to generate such a context. The participants ought to know each other fairly well, meeting regularly and learning to trust each other – not only in the seminar but outside it, perhaps in schools or in the pub afterwards, or in each other's homes during some informal socializing. It helps such informality to share drinks, or food, or coffee; to have the chairs so positioned that people are comfortable and in touch with each other; in general to produce an atmosphere of safety, trust and close communication. Much turns here, of course, on whether the seminar leader is the sort of person who can use humour and enthusiasm and other personal characteristics – in particular, perhaps, the willingness to be vulnerable and admit to his or her own prejudices – to engender the right atmosphere.

Serious intellectual discussion is a sophisticated business: not everyone (not even everyone with a university degree!) is at home with it. Various teaching techniques may help. Usually to leave the discussion entirely open places too much of a burden on people: getting individuals to give a five- or ten-minute talk to introduce the topic is a very useful device (with perhaps someone to answer it just as briefly). Longer written work comes best after discussion. Or we may ask ourselves to criticize a particular paper, like the short chapters in this book. Or we may start with a particular incident at school, and try to generalize the incident so as to grasp the main points relevant to the topic. How far one should structure the discussion must depend on how easy or difficult we find it to discuss within the group: generally speaking, the move should be from a fairly tight or semi-formal structure at the start, towards a looser framework of general discussion when the participants become more secure and sophisticated in their communication.

It is throughout very important to *connect* what might be called the 'practical' aspects of the topic – a particular school experience, for instance – with the 'theoretical', and move back and forth from one end of the scale to the other. In this book most of the material is concerned more with the 'theoretical' end of the scale, for the simple reason that particular personal experiences can only be produced by the individuals themselves, whereas some of the major 'theoretical' points about concepts and values can be made on paper. But in reality the 'theory'–'practice' distinction does not really work for education (as it does not for being a parent, or personal relationships, or for many other contexts): it is throughout a matter of monitoring one's own concepts, reactions, attitudes, values and opinions. That is why a context of trust and close communication is so important.

I have said quite a lot on these points elsewhere (see Wilson, 1975), which it would be inappropriate to repeat here. But the general problem of the kind of discussion, teaching and learning which is needed, and the ways in which it can be forwarded, is so important for education generally as to merit some discussion in the seminar group itself. If things go badly (or perhaps also if they go well) in the group, we need to take a hard look at it: we have to monitor our own progress as well as just taking a set of topics on board as part of a fixed syllabus. For no serious progress can be made with the topics unless we get the conditions of discussion right.

In recent years there has been a tendency to replace the usual process of seminar discussion with other forms: role-play, simulation situations, visual aids, case histories, critical incidents, workshops and so on. As introductions to serious discussion, or what might be called 'stimulus material', these may indeed be useful: many people may find it difficult to enter immediately into sophisticated intellectual argument about what are, admittedly, difficult problems. Here again each institution will use the methods and contexts which seem most suitable. But we should guard against their excessive use, particularly since time is short; there is a danger that the really hard and basic questions may not even be asked, or not faced squarely; that they may be squeezed out and overwhelmed by these other activities which, whilst they may be popular and useful, may also lack intellectual rigour. We need to make space for *hard argument*, something that can only occur in a seminar where anyone can speak with no holds barred. It is with this sort of context, at least, that this book is concerned and has to be used.

III   RELATIONSHIP TO EXPERIENCE

Of course both tutors and students will want, not just to consider these issues in the abstract, but to relate them to their practical experience. That is part of what it is to be or become a good teacher or educator, a good 'reflective practitioner' (to use a popular contemporary phrase). Here there is one very important point that needs to be made, when we think of the relationship of reflection about concepts and values to our experience. It is that 'experience' (whether in school, as a practising teacher, or elsewhere) does not come in packaged chunks, to be absorbed as we absorb sunlight or vitamins. It is mediated and indeed *constituted by* the concepts, values and beliefs which we *bring to* it. We enter upon, say, the experience of classroom teaching with a set of beliefs and expectations (sometimes unconscious) which determine what we notice in the classroom and what we fail to notice, what aspects of the students we consider important and what unimportant. 'Experience' in the sense of simply *being* in a particular situation will teach us nothing. (People had, and still have, plenty of 'experience', in this sense, of women or Jews or heretics, yet were able to keep women in subjection, persecute Jews, and burn heretics at the stake.) Everything turns on whether we sophisticate and reflect intelligently on the concepts and values which we bring to our 'experience'; or, more precisely, on the kind of 'experience' we have, which will inevitably be dictated by what we bring to it.

It follows from this that both before and during our practical 'experience' we have to make ourselves aware of the general attitudes, concepts and values which we bring to it. In other words, we have to be able to consider our problems from a point of view which may, to some temperaments, seem 'abstract' or 'academic' or even 'unreal'. Very often, and not least in teacher education, we are anxious to 'get on with something practical', to initiate ourselves into 'the system', to 'stop arguing about academic matters' and 'immerse ourselves in the real world'. Of course we need the experience, in order to make the principles clear to ourselves and learn how to apply them to particular cases; but we must not run away with the idea that learning to be a teacher (or, more widely, an educator – an important difference) is just a matter of 'experience' plus the learning of a few practical 'skills'. As with being a good parent, it is much more a matter of our own personalities, characters and virtues; and these have to be improved both by reflection about ourselves and our concepts, and by testing this reflection in practice.

I make no apology, then, for facing the reader with these issues head on, as it were, in a form which demands his intellectual concentration and willingness to reason about them at a high level of generality. The point here is not to 'preserve academic standards' or 'maintain a high level of scholarship': it is simply that these are, in reality, the issues which any intelligent 'experience' and/or any serious intellectual thought and reflection forces a serious and honest person to confront. They are not 'abstract' or 'academic' issues which can be reflected upon as a luxury, so to speak, alongside the 'practical' business of learning to teach: they are the very stuff of education, which we turn away from only at our peril. Certainly they are difficult and demanding; but so is education, if it is conducted seriously. If anyone merely wants to 'fit into the system', or just go through the motions of talking about the issues because it is expected, this book is not for them.

That does not mean, of course, that students should not make as much use as possible of the different kinds of experience and conversations they have at school. Here they will often find, unsurprisingly, that the teachers are so preoccupied with day-to-day decisions and difficulties that they do not have much time for considering the basic issues. Bridging the gap between this preoccupation and the basic issues is extremely difficult; and there will be a temptation either to dismiss the school culture as insufficiently 'intellectual' or, more probably, to dismiss the intellectual challenge of the issues as insufficiently 'practical'. We have to avoid both temptations, and it is a large part of the tutor's job to help students to connect the two cultures. This is partly a matter of skilful administration, by which reflection and practice are brought together at the right time and in the right place; but it is also a matter of ensuring that students do not opt unilaterally for one or the other culture because of their own personal preferences.

There is not much that can be said in a book of this kind which can be helpful here: every institution will have its own ways of trying to solve the problem. But it is perhaps worth saying that (1) in consideration of any basic issue – the chapters in this book, for instance – both tutors and students should always have in mind the general question 'How can our understanding of this basic issue be applied to school practice?'; and (2) in the experience of any piece of school practice, they should always ask 'To what basic issue does this practice lead our thoughts?' Acquiring the *habit* of relating the two can achieve a great deal.

Questions for discussion

CHAPTERS 1–4   THE ENTERPRISE OF EDUCATION

1. What does the word 'educate' mean? How does it differ from 'indoctrinate', 'socialize', 'teach', and other terms?
2. To what extent, and in what way(s), is the concept marked by 'educate' contestable?
3. What does 'learn' mean? What attitudes, virtues and other qualities are necessary for learning?
4. Is education inevitably bound up with politics? If so, in what ways? If not, why is it commonly thought to be?
5. What qualities are central to being a good educator? How could these qualities be identified and increased?
6. What kind of teacher education do you think is best?
7. How do teachers educate pupils other than in classroom periods?
8. Should education be chiefly concerned with (a) the intellect, or (b) character?
9. What (in your experience) are the chief enemies or hindrances to education in schools today?
10. If teachers are to be regarded as true professionals, what should their expertise consist of?

CHAPTER 5   THE CURRICULUM

1. What is a sensible meaning for 'curriculum'? How far is what most pupils need met by *curriculum* (as against other aspects of school life)?
2. What categories should we use when laying out different parts of the curriculum?
3. Two distinctions: (a)   What is useful for extrinsic ends.
                       (b)   what is valuable in itself.

(i)   what is important for local conditions.

(ii)   what is important for the individual in him or herself.

How does one argue for either side of either distinction?

4. What is particularly important, especially under (b) and (ii), about your teaching subject?
5. Why should not people specialize if they want to?
6. Who should control the curriculum (that is, what expertise is needed for making the decisions)?
7. What parts of the curriculum can we reasonably compel pupils to engage in?
8. Do you believe in across-the-board skills (e.g. 'thinking skills', 'creativity', 'problem-solving', etc.)?
9. How do your views about the human condition affect your views about the curriculum?
10. What subjects are really important for human beings as such, and what are less central?

CHAPTER 6   TEACHING A SUBJECT

1. How far are school subjects (a) things that exist in their own right, or (b) social constructions which can be altered at will?
2. What is a 'form of thought'? Is this a helpful notion for the curriculum?
3. What light does the notion of 'forms of thought' shed on your teaching subject?
4. What does the title of your teaching subject (a) include and (b) exclude?
5. What could be meant by 'integrating' school subjects? Do you approve?
6. Are some school subjects more wide-ranging than others?
7. How would one argue for one or another interpretation of a subject title (e.g. 'French', 'English', 'science' etc.)?
8. Are there educational objectives which do not fall within any subject title?
9. Can anything helpfully be said about methods of teaching a subject in general, i.e. without reference to the nature of the subject?
10. Are all subjects equally important?

CHAPTER 7   MAKING SUBJECTS INTERESTING

1. What is particularly attractive about your own teaching subject?
2. How can you make this visible to your pupils?
3. Is your teaching subject suitable for all pupils?
4. Are there ways of teaching your subject, or of pupils learning it, outside the classroom?

5. What virtues or abilities are required to perform well in your subject?
6. What peculiar difficulties are there in learning your subject?
7. What sort of 'motivation' do you consider appropriate and effective for the learning of subjects in secondary schools?
8. What would be the ideal way of examining or assessing progress in your subject?
9. How did you personally first become attached to your teaching subject?
10. What is the connection between your subject and life in general?

CHAPTER 8   DISCIPLINE AND AUTIIORITY

1. Would you rather go into school, as a teacher, (a) with a claim to some sort of impersonal authority (if so, of what sort?), or (b) more as a missionary or salesperson, displaying your wares but not exercising any authority or power to make the pupils buy them? Say how you *feel* about either option. Justify *intellectually* your choice between the two.
2. Are the teachers in your school clear about the concepts of discipline and authority? If not, why not? What sort of ideology do they have in this area?
3. What rules are in force in your school? What sanctions are attached to them? Are they generally obeyed? Are they obeyed for the right reasons?
4. What powers (a) do you actually have as a teacher, (b) ought you to have?
5. Think of some recent incidents in your school. What light do they shed on the way in which teachers handle the problems of discipline?
6. What personal hang-ups do you think make it hard for you to keep order?
7. How far are your problems in maintaining discipline (a) within yourself, (b) due to the system of discipline and sanctions in school, (c) due to the pupils themselves?
8. How far does the notion of a contract between pupils, teachers and parents help with discipline?
9. What would you do to educate the *pupils'* understanding of these concepts?
10. IIow far should pupils be encouraged to run their own school?

CHAPTER 9   PSE AND MORAL EDUCATION

1. Must moral education or PSE rest on some particular set of moral values?
2. In what ways is education in morality (a) like, (b) unlike, education in other forms of thought?
3. What counts as a good reason in moral (political) decisions?

4. Are there right answers to moral problems?
5. Should we teach moral decision-making to pupils in class?
6. What can be done about moral education outside the classroom?

CHAPTER 10   PASTORAL CARE

1. How would you organize 'pastoral care' in a secondary school?
2. What arrangements in schools would make pupils feel psychologically secure and self-confident?
3. How far, and in what ways, should schools be integrated with the local community?
4. Should teachers be *in loco parentis* (in the place of a parent)?

CHAPTER 11   SELECTION AND GROUPING

1. Do you approve of 'mixed ability' teaching?
2. What is the best criterion for selection in secondary schools?
3. How far should parental choice control the admission of pupils to schools?
4. What are the arguments for and against a comprehensive school system?
5. What are the dangers and advantages of independent schools?
6. Should pupils be grouped according to age or according to attainment?
7. Do some school subjects require a different criterion for selection and pupil-grouping from other subjects?
8. What can be done to prevent less able pupils feeling that they are 'failures'?
9. Do you approve of special schools for gifted children?
10. How would you organize and administer a school system for your local area?

CHAPTER 12   COMPETITION

1. What would be an adequate definition of 'competition'?
2. Is competition logically required for certain activities?
3. Could any society exist without competition?
4. How far should examination or assessment procedures be competitive?
5. How much emphasis would you put on achievement in education?
6. What non-competitive activities are important for pupils?
7. Are some pupils low achievers in general? Or is everyone 'good at' something?
8. How can one make less able children feel valued?
9. What emotions are relevant to competition?
10. How can pupils learn to come to terms with their own success and failure?

CHAPTER 13   EQUALITY

1. In what ways is equality different from justice?
2. What human differences are particularly relevant to education?
3. What could be meant by 'equal opportunity' in education?
4. What could be meant by 'equality of outcome' in education?
5. Can the notion of equality help us to define the aims of education?
6. In what sense, if any, are all human beings 'equal'?
7. Does the notion of equality conflict with the notion of excellence?
8. Adults seem to treat children as minors, not as equals: is this justified?
9. Is equality an educational or a political notion?
10. In what ways, in your teaching, would you treat pupils (a) equally and (b) unequally?

CHAPTER 14   DIVERSITY I: MULTICULTURAL EDUCATION AND SPECIAL NEEDS

1. We currently single out certain classes of 'victims' under such headings as 'sexism', 'racism', etc. Which classes *ought* to be singled out, in your view?
2. In dealing with different classes, do you want (a) to stress the differences, or (b) to play them down?
3. Just what do we mean by 'prejudice'?
4. If we aim to educate people, what do we do if some culture (creed, class, race, etc.) has norms/values/practices which are counter-educational (e.g. a tradition of magic or witchcraft as against science)? Or if it has a tradition/practice which goes against our moral principles (e.g. female circumcision)?
5. Does more 'integration' or mixing of various ethnic groups, creeds, cultures, etc. in itself produce more understanding and tolerance?
6. On what should pupils base their self-confidence, or self-esteem, or sense of 'identity'? How far should their own culture and practices form part of these?
7. How far should pupils be encouraged to see themselves primarily as members of 'society' (and, if so, of what 'society')? And how far as autonomous, being able to stand back from 'society' and criticize it and rise above it?
8. What *structure* in schools would be best to prevail over various kinds of prejudice or irrationality?
9. What criteria would you use to identify a 'special need'?
10. What cases of 'special needs' should be integrated into normal schools?

CHAPTER 15   DIVERSITY II: GENDER

1. Granted physical differences between males and females, what implications do those differences have for education?
2. Are there differences of ability between the two sexes? How would one confirm or disprove this?
3. Are there differences of attitude/interest/motivation between the two sexes? How would one verify this?
4. How far do you regard arguments from evolution or biology as persuasive in respect of sex differences between human beings?
5. It is believed by many psychiatrists that differences of relationships between male children and female children and their fathers and mothers produce different 'case histories' in the case of each sex. Do you agree? What sort of evidence would you accept for or against this?
6. How far do you think that non-negotiable biological differences (e.g. in producing and bearing children) affect attitudes in either sex?
7. Do you think that 'society' (and what particular societies?) (a) reinforces sex differences, and/or (b) actually creates them?
8. What should 'equal opportunity' mean for men and women?
9. 'Women should have more power.' What kinds of 'power' are there, and which are most important?
10. How do pupils of different sexes group themselves, and behave, in your school? At what ages? With what results?

References

Austin, J.L. (1961) *Philosophical Papers*. Oxford: Oxford University Press.
Hamlyn, D. (1978) *Experience and the Growth of Understanding*. London: Routledge and Kegan Paul.
Hare, R.M. (1977) Opportunities for what? *Oxford Review of Education*, **3**(3).
Hare, R.M. (1981) *Moral Thinking*. Oxford: Oxford University Press.
Hirst, P.H. (ed.) (1983) *Educational Theory and Its Foundation Disciplines*. London: Routledge.
Hirst, P.H. and Peters, R.S. (eds) (1970) *The Logic of Education*. London: Routledge and Kegan Paul.
Peters, R.S. (1966) *Ethics and Education*. London: Allen & Unwin.
Plato (1970) *Republic* (ed. R.M. Hare and D.A. Russell). London: Sphere Books.
Wilson, J. (1975) *Educational Theory and the Preparation of Teachers*. Windsor: NFER.
Wilson, J. (1977) *Philosophy and Practical Education*. London: Routledge and Kegan Paul.
Wilson, J. (1979) *Preface to the Philosophy of Education*. London: Routledge and Kegan Paul.

Further reading

Each topic could in principle have a whole bibliography attached to it, but there are good reasons for giving only a short reading list here. Time on all teacher education courses is short: many books on education date very quickly: and tutors will have their own ideas about what is most suitable for their own students (much may depend on local conditions, and on the direction which seminars and other discussions take). Rather than try to single out the best specialized works on each topic, I give here a number of books in which the enterprise of education and the most important topics are discussed from a general viewpoint. These contain plenty of references to more specialized works. I have chosen those which seem to me clearly written and of more than ephemeral value.

Badcock, C.R. (1983) *Madness and Modernity*. Oxford: Blackwell.
Barrow, R. (1976) *Common Sense and the Curriculum*. London: Allen & Unwin.
Beck, J. (1998) *Morality and Citizenship in Education*. London: Cassell.
Dearden, R.F., Hirst, P.H. and Peters, R.S. (eds) (1972) *Education and the Development of Reason*. London: Routledge.
Hamlyn, D. (1978) *Experience and the Growth of Understanding*. London: Routledge and Kegan Paul.
Hare, R.M. (1981) *Moral Thinking*. Oxford: Oxford University Press.
Hare, R.M. (1992) *Essays in Religion and Education*. Oxford: Oxford University Press.
Haydon, G. (1998) *Teaching About Values*. London: Cassell.
Hirst, P.H. (ed.) (1983) *Educational Theory and Its Foundation Disciplines*. London: Routledge.
Hirst, P.H. and Peters, R.S. (eds) (1970) *The Logic of Education*. London: Routledge and Kegan Paul.
Kant, I. (1960) *Education*. Michigan: University of Michigan Press.
Loukes, H., Cowell, B. and Wilson, J. (1983) *Education: An Introduction*. Oxford: Martin Robertson.
Morris, B. (1972) *Objectives and Perspectives in Education*. London: Routledge and Kegan Paul.
Peters, R.S. (1966) *Ethics and Education*. London: Allen & Unwin.
Peters, R.S. (ed.) (1970) *The Concept of Education*. London: Routledge and Kegan Paul.

Peters, R.S. (ed.) (1973) *The Philosophy of Education*. Oxford: Oxford University Press.

Plato (1970) *Republic* (ed. R.M. Hare and D.A. Russell). London: Sphere Books.

Richards, J.R. (1980) *The Sceptical Feminist*. London: Routledge and Kegan Paul.

Walsh, P. (1998) *Education and Meaning*. London: Cassell.

Wilson, B. (ed.) (1975) *Education, Equality and Society*. London: Allen & Unwin.

Wilson, J. (1975) *Educational Theory and the Preparation of Teachers*. Windsor: NFER.

Wilson, J. (1977) *Philosophy and Practical Education*. London: Routledge and Kegan Paul.

Wilson, J. (1981) *Discipline and Moral Education*. Windsor: NFER.

Wilson, J. (1990) *A New Introduction to Moral Education*. London: Cassell.

Wilson, J. (1995) *Love Between Equals*. London: Macmillan.

Yudkin, M. (ed.) (1969) *General Education*. London: Penguin.

Index